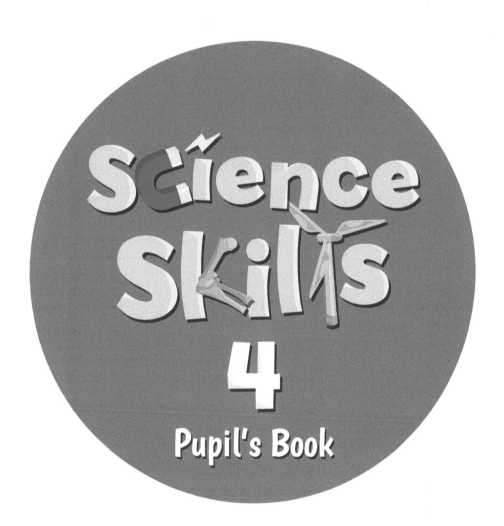

Science Skills

4

Pupil's Book

by

Kevin Walker

CAMBRIDGE
UNIVERSITY PRESS

SCIENCE SKILLS 4

Contents

Projects and experiments	Documentaries
· Create a 3D body systems mural · Check vital signs	· Respiration and circulation
· Create a healthy habits awareness campaign · Learn about the negative effects of not getting enough rest	· Healthy and unhealthy habits
· Make wildlife park signs about vertebrates and invertebrates · Observe the effect of carbon dioxide on litmus paper	· Marine invertebrates
· Create a quiz about plant reproduction and nutrition · Observe plant respiration	· Plant reproduction
· Make a materials classroom display · Predict if objects will sink or float	· Forces
· Create a slide presentation on simple and complex machines · Make a lever	· Inventions that changed the world

More hands on ...  Page 90

WELCOME TO CAMBRIDGE SCIENCE SKILLS

Welcome to the amazing world of natural science. In this book, you will:

make a
3D model

become a wildlife park warden

learn about recyclable materials

create a health awareness campaign

organise a table quiz

find machines in your neighbourhood

You will also find out:

- what your respiratory rate is
- how to detect oxygen
- how to see the oxygen plants release
- whether certain objects sink or float
- how levers work.

HOW DO OUR BODY SYSTEMS WORK?

Look and see ...

What do we get from the air that helps us live?

How do you feel after running around for a long time?

What body systems are the people in these photos using?

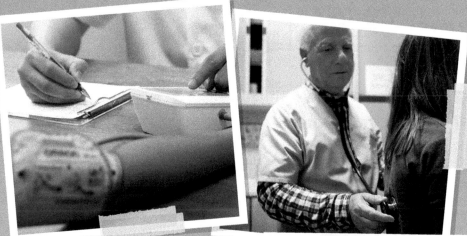

What is happening
in each photo? Why?

Investigate

In this unit, you will create a 3D body systems mural. To do this, you will:

- work in groups to create a mural.
- learn more about the respiratory system, including how we get oxygen from the air.
- learn more about the circulatory system, including how the heart pumps blood.
- present each part of the mural to the class as a group.

WHY ARE BODY SYSTEMS *VITAL?*

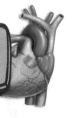

By the end of this lesson, you will know what the main body systems are.

Body systems are groups of organs which work together to perform a specific job. For example, the locomotor system allows us to move around from one place to another. Do you remember what each one of these systems allows us to do?

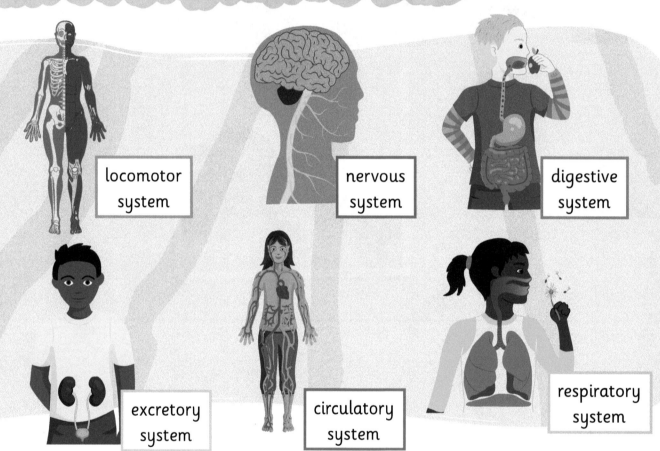

locomotor system

nervous system

digestive system

excretory system

circulatory system

respiratory system

Body systems are sometimes called 'vital systems'. In English, the word *vital* means 'absolutely necessary' and 'essential for life'.

Investigate — STAGE 1

- In groups of four, join four sheets of A2 card together. Lay out the sheets horizontally and tape them together from behind.

- One member of the group lies down on the long piece of paper with their arms, legs and fingers spread out.

- The other group members trace the outline of their body.

VITAL SIGNS

Hands on...

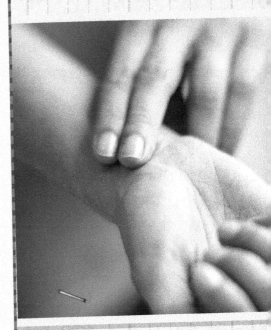

Before you start

The doctor checks our vital signs to make sure that our body systems are working properly. You can also check some of the vital signs of your classmates.

Materials

pencil, notebook, digital thermometer, clock or stopwatch

Method

1 Work with a partner. Copy and complete the table in your notebook:

	Body temperature	Pulse (beats per minute)	Respiratory rate (breaths per minute)
Your name	..... °C	..... bpm	..... bpm
Your partner's name	..... °C	..... bpm	..... bpm

2 Measure your partner's body temperature using the thermometer. Make a note of it in your notebook.

3 Measure your partner's pulse. Place your forefinger and middle finger on your partner's wrist and count the pulsations for one minute. Write it down.

4 Finally, measure your partner's respiratory rate. Using the clock, count how many times they breathe in and out in one minute.

5 Then, it is your turn to be the patient.

6 Run once around the school patio and repeat the process.

Conclusions

Are your results very different from your partner's?

How have the results changed after you ran?

> My partner had a *higher / lower* body temperature than me.

> My pulse was *quicker / slower* than my partner's.

HOW DO YOU GET OXYGEN FROM THE AIR?

The **respiratory system** is a group of organs that perform respiration. **Respiration** is another way of saying 'breathing'. In respiration, we breathe in air which contains oxygen and we breathe out carbon dioxide. Our body needs oxygen to perform nutrition and give us energy.

Do you know that one of your lungs is smaller than the other? Find out why!

1 Air enters our body through the **mouth** and the **nose**.

nose

mouth

2 The air passes through a tube called the **trachea,** to two large tubes called the **bronchi**.

trachea

bronchi

lungs

3 The bronchi lead to two large organs which are responsible for breathing: the **lungs.**

On average, a child of your age takes about 1200 breaths per hour. So, how many times do you breathe in a day?

diaphragm

4 Below the lungs, there is a muscle called the **diaphragm**. This muscle helps the lungs to perform respiration. When it **contracts**, air is drawn into[1] our lungs.

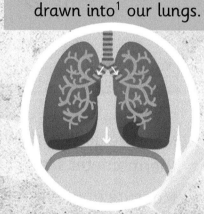

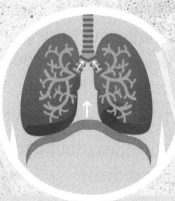

5 When the diaphragm **relaxes**, air is expelled from our lungs.

Oxygen goes in, carbon dioxide comes out

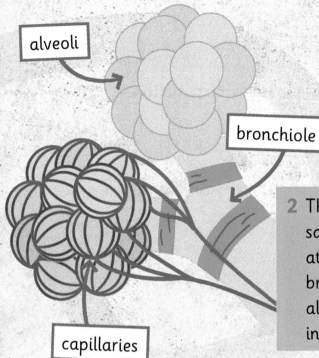

alveoli

bronchiole

capillaries

By the end of this lesson, you will know how many bronchioles are in each lung.

1 The bronchi divide into smaller tubes inside the **lungs**. These tubes are called **bronchioles**.

2 There are tiny air sacs called **alveoli** at the end of each bronchiole. The alveoli are covered in **capillaries**.

Did you know there are about 30,000 bronchioles in each lung? Each one is about as thick as a hair.

3 In the alveoli, the **oxygen** from the air we breathe in passes into the blood. The **carbon dioxide** our body produces leaves the blood through the alveoli, and is expelled when we breathe out.

Try this ...

The amount of air we can fit in our lungs is called our **lung capacity**.

Get into groups of five. Each pupil has a balloon. Everyone takes a deep breath and blows into the balloon until they run out of air. Observe the different lung capacities.

Investigate STAGE 2

- Make a model of the respiratory system using plasticine or mixed materials, such as balloons, plastic bags, straws, cardboard rolls ...
- Attach your model to the body outline using glue, tape or staples.
- Label each part. You can make labels using card.

[1]*to draw into*: to pull in

IS THERE A PUMP IN YOUR BODY?

The **circulatory system** is a group of organs that performs **circulation**. This is the process by which blood is moved around the body.

Blood is like a delivery system. It carries oxygen, water and other nutrients to all the cells in the human body. It also carries carbon dioxide to the lungs, from where it is exhaled. The main organs in the circulatory system are the **heart** and the **blood vessels** (**veins**, **arteries** and **capillaries**).

If you laid out all the blood vessels in your body in a line, how long would that line be? Find out!

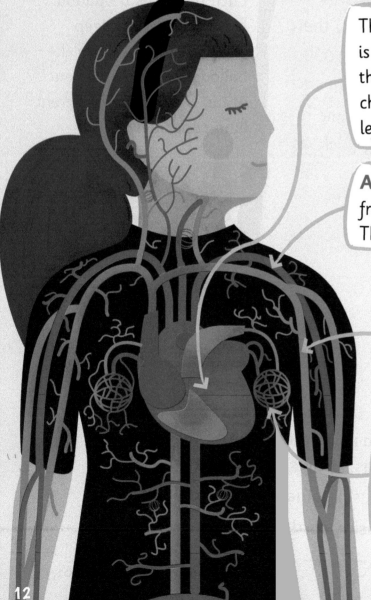

The **heart** is a muscular organ. Its function is to pump blood around the body through the blood vessels. It is divided into four chambers: the left and right **atriums** and left and right **ventricles**.

Arteries are blood vessels that carry blood from the heart to the rest of the body. The blood in the arteries is rich in oxygen.

Veins are the blood vessels that carry blood back to the heart. The blood in the veins is low in oxygen and contains carbon dioxide.

Capillaries are the smallest blood vessels. They connect the veins and the arteries.

Pump it!

The heart is the pump of the human body. It can never stop pumping because our body is in constant need of oxygen, which is like fuel[1] for the muscles and organs.

By the end of this lesson, you will know how veins and arteries are connected.

1 Deoxygenated[2] blood enters the heart through the **right atrium**. It then passes to the **right ventricle**, where it is pumped into the **lungs**.

2 In the lungs, the blood passes through the **alveoli** and picks up **oxygen** and gets rid of[3] **carbon dioxide**.

3 The oxygenated[4] blood is then pumped into the **left atrium** and passes into the **left ventricle**, from where it is pumped around the body through the arteries.

Inside the heart, there are valves which open to let the blood pass through and close to stop it flowing backwards.

right atrium

lungs

left ventricle

Find another heart hidden in the unit.

Investigate STAGE 3

- Make a model of the heart using plasticine or mixed materials.
- Attach the model to the outline of the body and label the different parts of the heart.
- To represent the veins, you can use thin blue ribbon. To represent the arteries, you can use thin red ribbon. Glue the ribbon to the outline.

[4]**oxygenated:** rich in oxygen
[3]**to get rid of:** to remove
[2]**deoxygenated:** with the oxygen removed
[1]**fuel:** source of energy, material that is burnt to produce heat or power

1 🎧 **Listen and match the names with the letters in your notebook.**

Brian   Dermot   Aideen   Mary   Brigid   Fergus

WHAT'S INSIDE US?

2 **Complete the sentences in your notebook using the words *after* or *before*.**

a My pulse was quicker ..... I ran around the school patio.

b Air passes through the trachea ..... passing into the bronchi.

c The blood is oxygenated ..... passing through the alveoli.

d The blood is deoxygenated ..... passing through the alveoli.

1 Identify the parts of the circulatory system. Write them in your notebook.

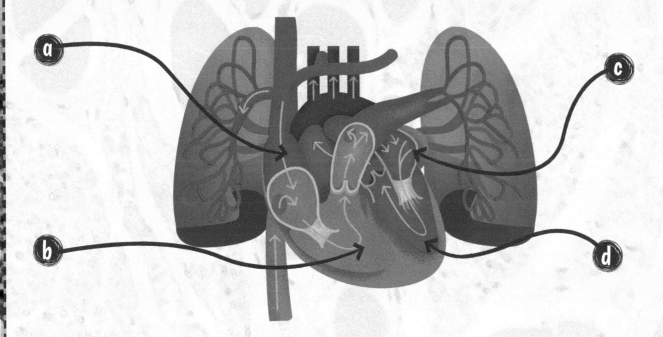

2 🎧 Listen and choose *a*, *b* or *c*.

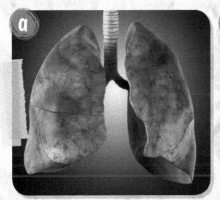
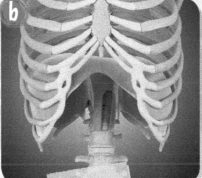
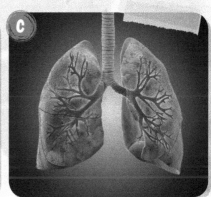

Investigate FINALE

- It is time to present your body systems mural to the rest of your class.
- Each group member chooses one body system to present.
- Practise what you are going to say before class.
- You can make prompt cards to help you.

Assessment link

Go to page 78 for more activities.

This is the ... system.

The ... system has ... main parts.

2

HOW ARE YOU FEELING?

Look and see ...

Have you ever had these symptoms before?

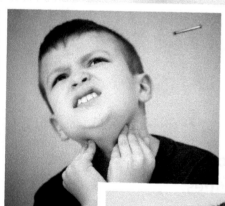

When you are ill, what do you do to get better?

Which of these are healthy habits and which are unhealthy?

Investigate

In this unit, you will create a healthy habits awareness campaign for your class. To do this, you will:

- study some common illnesses and how to prevent them.
- learn about some healthy habits that are easy to follow.
- identify some unhealthy habits and dangerous behaviours.
- find out about some first-aid techniques.

WHAT'S CHICKEN POX?

Our body systems never stop working. However, sometimes our body can be affected by **illness**. Common illnesses are caused by microbes called **viruses** and **bacteria**. We get ill because these microbes enter our body through the mouth, nose or a wound. Some illnesses are not very serious, but it is important to know what the symptoms are.

Common illnesses

The common cold

This is one of the most common illnesses. It is caused by a **virus**. The common cold affects the **upper respiratory system**. The best way to stop it spreading is by washing your hands. Symptoms include:

- ☐ sore throat
- ☐ blocked or runny nose
- ☐ sneezing and coughing
- ☐ low fever
- ☐ mild body aches
- ☐ symptoms start slowly

The flu

The flu, short for *influenza*, is also a virus. Like the common cold, it affects our **respiratory system**. However, the flu is a stronger illness than the cold, its symptoms begin more quickly and it causes higher fever and stronger body aches.

Chicken pox

This illness is also caused by a virus. It mainly affects children. The main symptom of chicken pox is a **rash** in the form of red spots on the skin. Chicken pox is **contagious**, so when you catch it, the best thing is to stay at home and not go to school.

When did you last have a cold? How did you feel?

Find out how chicken pox is spread.

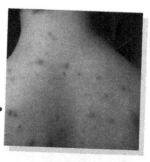

Another name for chicken pox is *varicella*.

Medicine

When we are ill, most times the best thing to do is rest in bed. However, we sometimes need to take medicine to help us **get better**. Some people need to take medicine every day to help their body function properly. For example, some people suffer from asthma and need to use an inhaler.

By the end of this lesson, you will know what the word *flu* is short for.

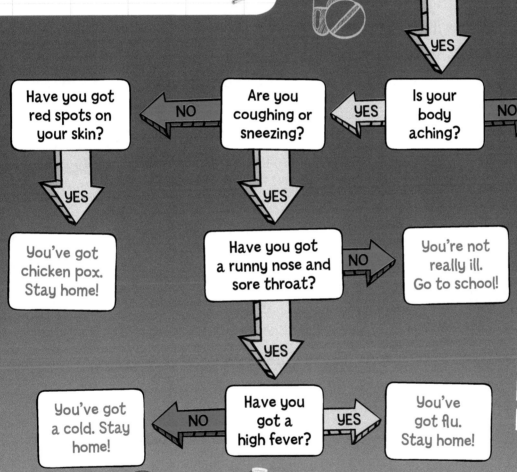

Are you feeling ill? — NO → Go to school!

YES ↓

Is your body aching? — NO → You've probably got an exam. Go to school!

YES ←

Are you coughing or sneezing? — NO → Have you got red spots on your skin?

YES ↓ (Have you got red spots on your skin?) → YES ↓ You've got chicken pox. Stay home!

Are you coughing or sneezing? YES ↓

Have you got a runny nose and sore throat? — NO → You're not really ill. Go to school!

YES ↓

Have you got a high fever? — YES → You've got flu. Stay home!

Have you got a high fever? — NO → You've got a cold. Stay home!

Are you feeling ill? With a partner, use this chart to see if you should go to school.

Investigate   STAGE 1

- Choose one of the three illnesses you have learnt about in this lesson.
- Find out about things we can do to prevent the illness and to get better.
- Choose one of the following formats: poster, video clip, audio file or slide presentation.
- Use the format to communicate a message about how to prevent the illness.

HOW MUCH EXERCISE DO YOU DO?

There are lots of things we can do to prevent illness and keep our bodies in good condition. We call these things **healthy habits**.

Balanced diet

A **balanced diet** contains foods from the different groups. By eating different foods, we get the different **nutrients** our body needs to function and stay healthy. We need to eat foods that are rich in these nutrients:

- Vitamins and minerals
- Carbohydrates
- Protein and iron
- Calcium
- Fats

Do you follow a balanced diet?

Vitamins and **minerals** help our bodies stay healthy in many different ways.

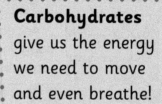

Carbohydrates give us the energy we need to move and even breathe!

Our muscles are made up of **proteins**. And we could not live without **iron** — it transports oxygen!

Fats help our brain and nerves, but we only need a little each day.

Your smile is all thanks to **calcium**, which forms our bones and teeth.

Our body gets energy by breaking down food into glucose, or blood sugar. **Diabetes** is a disease that affects how the body uses its blood sugar. Some people with diabetes can control their blood sugar through diet, while others must take medicine called **insulin** to stay healthy.

Can you name other illnesses connected to food or digestion?

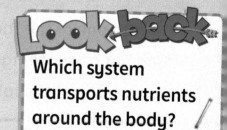

Look back

Which system transports nutrients around the body?

Exercise

Exercise is good for your **respiratory**, **circulatory** and **locomotor systems**. It is also good for your **mental health**! There are lots of activities to keep you active, for example dance lessons, athletics, gymnastics, football, karate lessons and fencing[1].

What activities do you do?

	Monday	Tuesday	Wednesday	Thursday ...
Me		Swimming	Bike ride with Dad	
Jane	Volleyball	Gymnastics		Play games in the park ...
Robert	Bike riding	Football	Fencing	

Design an exercise schedule for you and your friends so you are active each day. When you enjoy being active, it makes it more fun so be sure to include many different activities that you can do alone or in a group.

Investigate STAGE 2

- Choose either a balanced diet or exercise and find about that healthy habit.
- Choose a different format from the last lesson: poster, video clip, audio file or slide presentation.
- Communicate your message about the healthy habit.

[1] **fencing:** sport in which two people fight with swords

21

HOW CAN YOU FIGHT BAD BACTERIA?

By the end of this lesson, you will know what we use a stethoscope for.

Nutrition, exercise and rest are all important to prevent illness, but we must also keep clean and visit the doctor.

Personal hygiene

Bacteria are all around us. We cannot see them, but they are there. They are nothing to worry about if we take care of our personal hygiene. To do this, you should:

- brush your teeth after meals
- wash your hands before meals and after using the toilet
- have showers frequently
- use a tissue when you sneeze or blow your nose.

How many times a day do you brush your teeth?

Check-ups

It is a good idea to visit your doctor from time to time, even if there is nothing wrong with you. This visit is called a **check-up**. The doctor usually does the following things:

They measure your height and weight.

They look inside your ears, nose, mouth and throat.

They test your sight and hearing.

They measure your blood pressure using a sphygmomanometer.

They listen to your heart and lungs with a stethoscope[1].

Find a stethoscope hidden somewhere in this unit.

With a partner, take it in turns to be a doctor and a patient during a check-up. Measure your height and weight, then test your sight and hearing.

[1] **stethoscope**: instrument used by doctors to listen to someone's heartbeat or respiration.

22

HOW HEALTHY ARE YOUR SLEEP HABITS?

By the end of this lesson, you will know how long you should sleep every day.

Relax, chill out or *chillax*: these are some of the words we use to describe rest, something we should do every day.

Rest

Sometimes our body just needs to do nothing! Rest helps our body **recover** from our daily activity. The most important form of rest is **sleep**.

At what time do you go to bed?

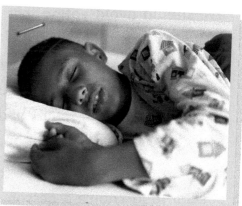

You need to get at least nine hours of sleep a night! Some people have trouble falling asleep or staying asleep. You will sleep easier and better if you have **healthy sleep habits**.

Having a routine that prepares your body to sleep is best. Relaxing before bed, avoiding distractions, and sleeping and waking at the same time are helpful.

It is important to sleep in the dark and in silence.

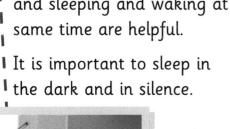

Do you do any of these before bed?

Investigate STAGE 3

- Choose one of the three healthy habits you have learnt about in these lessons.
- Find out about the healthy habit.
- Choose a different format from the last lesson: poster, video clip, audio file or slide presentation.
- Communicate your message about the healthy habit.

WHAT'S A COUCH POTATO?

By the end of this lesson, you will know what fast food does to our body.

Making healthy habits is important, but avoiding **unhealthy habits** is just as important.

We should avoid eating fast food. Fizzy drinks, crisps, sweets and chocolate can be eaten from time to time, but they are not good for you. Fast food can contain **high levels of sugar, salt** and **bad fats**. These are bad for our heart and can cause obesity and diabetes.

Find out about the two types of diabetes. Can people do anything to prevent or manage them?

We also use the word **diet** to talk about a special food choice a person limits themselves to for medical reasons or to lose weight. A certain weight doesn't mean health and happiness. Remember, everyone is unique. You should accept yourself and others **the way they are**.

Find out about different diets. Are all diets healthy?

If you stay up late, the next day you will be **tired** and will not be able to concentrate. Our eyes need rest, too, so we should **limit** the time we spend looking at **screens**.

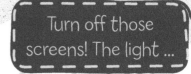

Turn off those screens! The light ...

makes it difficult to fall asleep

causes nightmares

makes it hard to stay asleep

makes you tired during the day

What happens if we don't sleep enough?

Sight problems

Headaches

Lower grades at school

More stress

Sadness

Someone who spends all day sitting on the sofa is called a *couch potato*.

Say 'no' to smoking!

Tobacco is a health hazard because it contains a very **addictive** chemical called **nicotine**. Once a person starts smoking, it can be very hard for them to stop. Smoking is **dangerous**.

It can...

- increase the risk of lung infections.
- damage your lungs and heart.
- cause many types of cancer.

Even if you don't smoke, you can be affected by **second-hand smoke** when a person smokes near you.

You should always **refuse** when someone offers you tobacco products.

> It will make my clothes smell bad!

> It will give me bad breath!

NO!

> I hate how it makes me look!

Taking care of YOU

Making healthy decisions will keep our bodies healthy, but our **mind** must be healthy, too.

- Be around positive people.
- Participate in helpful activities.
- Resolve conflicts peacefully.
- Reflect on how other people may feel.

This is called **empathy**. We all have our own possibilities and limits, and these should always be respected.

Growing up can be exciting because you can start making your **own decisions** and acting more **responsibly**. Building **trust** is also important.

How do your decisions affect you and the people around you?

Investigate STAGE 4

- Find out more information about one of the unhealthy habits you have learnt about in this lesson.
- Choose a different format from the last lesson: poster, video clip, audio file or slide presentation.
- Communicate your message about the unhealthy habit.

How can you be more responsible and help more at home?

NO REST CAN'T PASS A TEST!

Hands On...

Before you start

When you do not sleep enough, you normally feel tired. You might also feel ill. Lack of sleep can negatively affect your mood, reaction time and concentration. It particularly affects your memory and ability to think. Simulate how difficult some tasks can be when your reaction time and concentration are negatively affected.

Predict what will happen

When you spin around, you won't be able to…

Materials

chalk or whiteboard markers, tennis ball

Method

1 In groups of six, stand in a circle. Each group throws a tennis ball to the person opposite them. Count how many times you can do this without dropping the ball. Record the number in a table.

2 Then, everyone spins around 15 times and repeats step 1. Count and record in a new row in the table.

3 In the same groups, take turns to do three maths problems on the whiteboard. The rest of the group time you.

4 Then, each person spins around 15 times and tries to do three more maths problems. The rest of the group times you and notes the mistakes you make.

Conclusions

Compare your results with a partner. Do you notice any similarities?

What do you think spinning around is similar to?

CAN YOU HELP PREVENT ACCIDENTS?

U

By the end of this lesson you will know how to prevent accidents.

Burns, cuts, broken bones – many of these **injuries** happen at home and can easily be **prevented**. If someone is injured or ill, there are also some actions you can take to help.

Being safe at home

We can prevent household injuries by being safer and more careful at home. For example, putting things away is easy and prevents accidents!

Who is being safe? What dangers can you find?

BE SAFE!
- Always look where you're walking.
- Fire, heat and electricity are dangerous. Only use them with an adult.
- Never use electrical devices near water.

What can you do to make your home safer?

First aid

First aid is the **help** we give **an ill or injured person** before they can see a doctor or get to a hospital. If someone …

… has burnt their hand, put it under cold running water.

… has a big cut, cover it with a cloth and apply pressure.

… has broken a bone, keep them still and support the injury.

REMEMBER!
- Always make sure it is safe for you to help first.
- Always try to get the help of an adult.
- If you think the injury is serious, call the emergency services.

1 🎧 **Listen and write the answers in your notebook.**

The Athletics Club

Example	Starts at:	4:30 pm
a	Children mainly do:	.....
b	When it rains, activities in the	.....
c	Children have to bring:	.....
d	Person who sometimes talks to the club:	.....
e	She is very:	.....

2 **Match and write the sentences in your notebook.**

a If someone appears to be seriously injured,

b If someone has broken a bone,

c If you have a cold,

d If you spend too much time looking at screens,

e If you stay up past your bed time,

your eyes get tired and you can get a headache.

you keep them still and support the injury.

you call the emergency services.

you are tired the next day.

you should rest.

1 Identify the illness in each picture and write it in your notebook.

2 Complete the sentences in your notebook.

a The common cold and the flu are caused by a ..... .

b People who suffer from ..... use an inhaler.

c First aid is the help we give someone ..... they can see a doctor.

d By eating different foods, we give our body the different ..... it needs.

Investigate FINALE

- It is time to present your healthy habits campaign to the rest of the class.

- Get into groups of four.

- Choose your favourite poster, video clip, audio file or slide presentation from each stage.

- Present the four messages, one after another.

Assessment link

Go to page 80 for more activities.

3

IS A SPONGE AN ANIMAL?

Look and see ...

Can you identify the five vertebrate groups?

Can you identify any of these invertebrates?

Song
Mammals, amphibians, birds, fish and reptiles

Can you name the groups they belong to?

DOCUMENTARY
Marine invertebrates

Investigate

In this unit, you will become wardens at a wildlife park and make signs with information about vertebrates and invertebrates for the visitors' centre. To do this, you will:

- learn about the five groups of vertebrates.
- understand the differences in how they perform the life processes of nutrition, reproduction and respiration.
- be able to classify invertebrates into six different groups, depending on their characteristics.

WHAT DO VERTEBRATES EAT?

This year, we will take a close look at animals. But first, let's revise some things you already know.

By the end of this lesson, you will know where the embryo develops in oviparous animals.

Vertebrates and invertebrates

Animals can be classified into **two different groups** depending on whether they have a **backbone**:

- Vertebrates have a backbone.
- Invertebrates do not have a backbone.

Nutrition

Animals are **consumers**. This means they eat other living things. Different vertebrates perform the life process of nutrition in different ways:

- **Carnivores** only eat other animals.
- **Herbivores** only eat plants.
- **Omnivores** eat both plants and other animals.

Respiration

All vertebrates need to take in oxygen and release carbon dioxide to live, but different vertebrates breathe in different ways:

- Some breathe with **lungs**.
- Others breathe through **gills**.
- Some even breathe through their **skin**.

Which animals breathe through their skin?

Reproduction

Vertebrates reproduce sexually, but they reproduce in different ways:

- **Viviparous** vertebrates give birth to live young. The embryo develops inside the female.
- **Oviparous** vertebrates lay eggs. The embryo grows outside the mother's body in an egg.

Find out how ovoviviparous animals reproduce.

Find a hatched egg hidden somewhere in this unit.

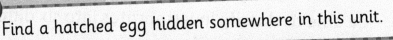

WHAT DO MEERKATS EAT?

Let's look at how **mammals** perform nutrition, respiration and reproduction.

Nutrition

Mammals can be **carnivores**, **herbivores** or **omnivores**.

Carnivores	Herbivores	Omnivores

Respiration

All mammals breathe using their **lungs**. For example, whales take in and expel air through their blowhole when they come to the surface of the water.

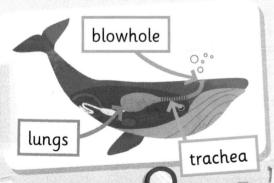

blowhole

lungs

trachea

Reproduction

Almost all mammals are **viviparous**. Mammals that lay eggs are called **monotremes**. The platypus and the echidna are examples of monotremes.

Respiration in whales is voluntary. They have to decide when they want to come to the surface to breathe.

Investigate   STAGE 1

- **Choose a mammal and research it. Make a sign.**
- **Include this information on the sign:**
  - the mammal's name
  - where and how it was born
  - the species
  - what it eats
  - some of its physical characteristics

WHAT DO SEAGULLS EAT?

By the end of this lesson, you will know why birds have different types of beaks.

Let's look at how **birds** perform nutrition, respiration and reproduction.

Nutrition

Like mammals, birds can be **carnivores**, **herbivores** or **omnivores**. We can tell what a bird eats by looking at its **beak**.

Hawks have a hooked beak for tearing meat.

Sparrows have cone-shaped beaks for eating seeds.

Woodpeckers have long, strong beaks for pecking into wood.

Hummingbirds have long, thin beaks for eating nectar.

Toucans have long, thick beaks for eating fruit.

Herons have long, pointed beaks for fishing and hunting.

Respiration

Like mammals, birds breathe using their **lungs**. Unlike mammals, birds do not have a diaphragm. Instead, they use **muscles** in their chest and muscles in their **air sacs** to inhale and exhale.

lungs

air sacs

trachea

Reproduction

Birds are **oviparous**. They lay eggs with hard shells. Most birds build **nests** to protect their eggs from predators and the weather. The adult birds incubate[1] their eggs.

[1] **to incubate:** to sit on eggs to keep them warm and make them hatch

34

HOW DO REPTILES REPRODUCE?

Let's look at how **reptiles** perform nutrition, respiration and reproduction.

By the end of this lesson, you will know how long sea turtles can hold their breath for.

Nutrition

Most reptiles are **carnivores**, but some are **omnivores** or **herbivores**. For example, most iguanas and tortoises are herbivores. Crocodiles and alligators are carnivores. They have long jaws[1] for catching their prey[2] and sharp teeth for cutting up meat.

Respiration

Like birds and mammals, all reptiles breathe using their **lungs**. Even aquatic reptiles like sea turtles must come to the surface to inhale air. However, sea turtles can hold their breath under water for as long as seven hours if they are resting.

lungs

trachea

Reproduction

Like birds, reptiles are **oviparous**. They lay their eggs on land. However, unlike birds, reptiles do not incubate their eggs. They do not nurture[3] their young either.

Investigate STAGE 2

- Choose one bird and one reptile.
- Prepare signs for each animal.
- For the bird, include a section on *beak type*.

[1]**jaw:** part of the mouth from where the teeth grow;
[2]**prey:** an animal that is hunted by another animal for food;
[3]**to nurture:** to feed, take care and help to develop

HOW DO AMPHIBIANS BREATHE?

By the end of this lesson, you will know how frogs catch their prey.

Let's look at how **amphibians** perform nutrition, respiration and reproduction.

Nutrition

Almost all adult amphibians are **carnivores**. They prey on small invertebrates, such as beetles, caterpillars, worms and spiders. Many amphibians catch invertebrates with their long tongues, which have a sticky tip. Tadpoles are herbivores.

Reproduction

Amphibians are **oviparous**. They lay soft eggs in water and do not incubate them. After emerging from the eggs, amphibians experience a transformation called **metamorphosis**.

Respiration

Amphibians change the way they perform respiration. Before metamorphosis, they take in oxygen from water using their **gills**. After metamorphosis, they take in oxygen from the air using their **lungs**. Adult amphibians can also breathe through their **moist skin**.

METAMORPHOSIS

lungs

Oxygen

Carbon dioxide

Look back

Can you remember the different stages of metamorphosis? Describe them to a partner using the picture.

gills

DO FISH SLEEP?

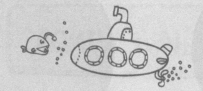

Let's look at how **fish** perform nutrition, respiration and reproduction.

Nutrition

The majority of fish are **carnivores**. However, some fish like the parrotfish are **herbivores**. Others, like the catfish, are **omnivores**.

Reproduction

Like amphibians, fish are **oviparous**. They lay their eggs underwater and do not incubate them.

Fish sleep with their eyes open because they do not have eyelids.

Respiration

Fish breathe through their **gills**.

The fish takes in water through its **mouth**. The water contains oxygen.

The water passes through **filaments** in the fish's **gills**. These filaments absorb oxygen from the water and move it into the blood.

Waste carbon dioxide is expelled together with the water through the **gills**.

Fish have to constantly take in fresh water to keep breathing.

Investigate   STAGE 3

- **Choose one amphibian and one fish.**
- **Prepare signs for each animal.**

DO ALL INSECTS HAVE WINGS?

About 97% of all animal species on the planet are **invertebrates**. Although there are millions of different invertebrate species, we classify them into **six main groups**: arthropods, molluscs, annelids, echinoderms, cnidarians and poriferans.

Arthropods

This is the largest group of invertebrates. Arthropods have an **exoskeleton**, a **segmented body** and **pairs of appendages**[1]. There are four main arthropod groups:

Insects

Insects have three main body sections: a **head**, a **thorax** and an **abdomen**. They have **six legs** and a pair of **antennae**. Some insects have **wings**. Examples: butterflies, ants and bees.

abdomen

thorax

Arachnids

Arachnids have two main body sections: an **abdomen** and a **cephalothorax**. They have **eight legs**. They do not have antennae or wings, and can have as many as eight eyes. Examples: spiders, scorpions and ticks.

abdomen

cephalothorax

Crustaceans

Most crustaceans have two main body sections: an **abdomen** and a **cephalothorax**. They have **10 legs**. Their front pair of legs are sometimes **claws**. They have two pairs of **antennae**. Examples: crabs and lobsters.

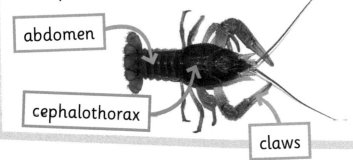

abdomen

cephalothorax

claws

Myriapods

Myriapods have two main sections: a head and a segmented body. Each segment of the body has one or two pairs of legs. They have one pair of **antennae**. Examples: millipedes and centipedes.

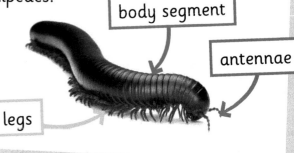

body segment

antennae

legs

Molluscs

Molluscs are the second largest group of invertebrates. They have a **soft body**. Some molluscs live **on land** and others live **in the water**. Almost all molluscs have a shell. They can be classified as follows:

By the end of this lesson, you will know how many legs ants have.

Gastropods

They have a large **muscular foot** that helps them move and most have a **shell**. Snails and slugs are gastropods.

Find out which gastropods do not have a shell.

Bivalves

The shell of a bivalve is divided into two parts, or *valves*. The **soft body** is inside the valves. Clams and oysters are bivalves.

Bivalves open their shell to eat, but close it when they are in danger.

Cephalopods

Cephalopods have an **internal shell**. They also have a **prominent head**. Instead of feet, they have **tentacles**. Octopuses, squids and cuttlefish are cephalopods.

Annelids

There are more than 17,000 species of annelids. Most live in water. Some, like the earthworm, live on land. Some annelids are parasites and live inside other animals. Their **body** is **long** and **soft**, and made up of **rings**. Earthworms and leeches are annelids.

Investigate — STAGE 4

- Investigate and prepare a sign for one of the three invertebrate groups on these pages:
  - arthropods
  - molluscs
  - annelids
- Include information on whether it is a *marine* or *terrestrial* invertebrate.

¹appendage: an arm, leg

WHAT IS A SEA CUCUMBER?

By the end of this lesson, you will know how sponges eat.

The animals in these three invertebrate groups all live in water.

Echinoderms

Echino means 'prickly' and *derm* means 'skin'. Most echinoderms have a **prickly structure** on the outside. They have an **internal skeleton** and **tube feet**, which help them attach to things and move around. Starfish, urchins and sea cucumbers are echinoderms.

Cnidarians

Cnidarians do not have a head or a brain, but they do have a **mouth**! It is their only body opening. The mouth is usually surrounded by **tentacles** containing venom, which they use to catch their prey. Jellyfish, sea anemones, coral and hydras are cnidarians.

Echinoderms can regenerate body parts if they lose them to a predator.

Poriferans

Poriferans live at the bottom of the ocean. They attach themselves to rocks and do not move around. There are pores on their bodies, which water passes through. This is how they get their food. **Sponges** are poriferans.

Investigate STAGE 5

- Investigate and prepare a sign for one of the three invertebrate groups on this page:
  - echinoderms
  - cnidarians
  - poriferans

BREATHING OUT

Hands On...

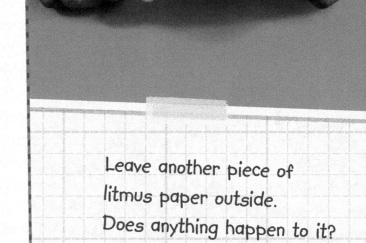

Before we start
Vertebrates and invertebrates inhale oxygen and exhale carbon dioxide. Carbon dioxide turns blue litmus paper red.

Materials
blue litmus paper, test tube

Method
1 Place the piece of litmus paper inside the test tube.

2 Blow into the test tube.

3 Observe what happens to the litmus paper.

Conclusions
What happened to the litmus paper?

What does this show? Talk to your partner.

Leave another piece of litmus paper outside. Does anything happen to it?

Can you think of another way to say 'breathe out' that begins with ex-?

Did you know that we breathe in about eight litres of air every minute?

1 Read the diary and write the missing words in your notebook.
Write one word for each line.

Example I am really enjoying our holiday in Ireland. We are in Cork at
a the moment. Today we ..... to a wildlife park. It was amazing.
b There ..... so many animals to see. There are pictures of them in
c my school books but it is very different to ..... them in real life.
d The ..... impressive animal that I saw was the capybara.
e It is the largest rodent in ..... world.
The only rodents I have ever seen are hamsters. The capybara
f was about 60 cm tall. It is classified as a .....
and it is covered in fur. We also saw Chilean flamingos.
g Their feathers ..... bright pink and each one of their legs is
h about 50 cm ..... . I am learning so much on this trip!

2 Complete these sentences in your notebook with the words *so* or *because*.
a A spider has eight legs ..... we classify it as an arachnid.
b We classify a wasp as an insect ..... it has three body sections, six legs
and wings.
c Mammals are called mammals ..... they have mammary glands.
d An oyster's shell is divided into two valves ..... we classify it as a bivalve.
e Hawks have sharp, pointed beaks ..... they can tear meat.

1 Copy and complete the table in your notebook.

breathe through their skin   breathe with gills   lay their eggs in water

carnivores   have different types of beak   herbivores   breathe with lungs

lay their eggs on land   monotremes   omnivores   oviparous

undergo metamorphosis   viviparous

Mammals	Birds	Reptiles	Amphibians	Fish
.....	.....	.....	.....	.....
.....	.....	.....	.....	.....
.....	.....	.....	.....	.....

2 Identify the invertebrate group or subgroup in each picture and write the names in your notebook.

Investigate   FINALE

- Find images of the animals you have written about. Include at least one image for each animal.
- Set up a visitors' centre. You can do this at your desk or in a corner of the classroom.
- Invite your classmates to come to your visitors' centre.
- Present your animals to them.

Assessment link
Go to page 82 for more activities.

4

WHY ARE PLANTS SO IMPORTANT?

Look and see ...

Can you name the main parts of a plant?

Can you name any parts of this flower?

Song
Without plants, we don't stand a chance!

How do we classify plants by their stems?

D▶CUMENTARY
Plant reproduction

Investigate

In this unit, you will become an expert in plant reproduction and nutrition, and put your classmates to the test with a table quiz. To do this you will:

- differentiate between sexual and asexual reproduction in plants.
- become familiar with the different parts of a flower.
- learn more about photosynthesis.
- understand the importance of plants for humans and all living things.

WHAT IS POLLINATION?

What are perfect flowers? Find out!

Plants reproduce in two different ways: **sexually** and **asexually**.

Sexual plant reproduction

A **flowering plant's** reproductive organs are in its **flowers**. Flowers can have **male parts, female parts** or **both**. The male parts are the **stamens** and the female part is the **pistil**. Sexual reproduction in plants takes place when male and female sex cells join together.

pollen

anther

stamen

filament

sepals

stigma

style

pistil

ovary

ovules

petal

Each **stamen** has two parts: a tube called a **filament** and an **anther**, where the male sex cells, or **pollen,** are made and stored.

The **pistil** is made up of:
- the **stigma**, which the pollen sticks to
- a tube called the **style**, which the pollen travels down
- the **ovary**, which contains the female sex cells, called **ovules**.

Animal pollination

1 Insects and small birds pick up pollen and transport it from the stamen to the pistil of the same plant or other plants.

2 Some of the pollen sticks to the stigma, from where it travels down through the style to the ovary and fertilises the ovules.

3 The fertilised ovule develops into a seed. When the flower withers[1] and dies, the seeds are spread and new plants grow.

Asexual plant reproduction

Non-flowering plants and some flowering plants reproduce asexually. This means there is no fusion of sex cells and **fertilisation does not take place**. There are different forms of asexual reproduction:

By the end of this lesson, you will know which animals pollinate.

Non-flowering plants

Non-flowering plants reproduce asexually with **spores**, as they do not produce seeds.

Look back

Can you name two non-flowering plants?

Flowering plants

Stolons

These are stems which grow horizontally along the ground. At certain intervals, roots are formed and a new shoot[2] grows upwards.

Stolons are also called 'runners'.

Rhizomes

These are similar to stolons, but they grow underground.

iris

Tubers

These are like thick stems which grow underground. Shoots grow out from the tuber.

potato

silverweed

Investigate — STAGE 1

- Get into groups of five and revise the content on these two pages.
- Each group member comes up with one question for the quiz.
- All the questions are written down on a piece of paper.

[1] **to wither:** to become dry and start to die; [2] **shoot:** new part that grows on a plant

WHAT DO PLANTS EAT?

Find out what type of 'troph' humans are.

Plants are **autotrophs**. This means they are able to make their own food. The process by which plants make their own food is called **photosynthesis**.

Photosynthesis

The **roots**, **stem** and **leaves** of a plant have different functions in photosynthesis.

3 From the stem, the water and minerals arrive in the **leaves**. Photosynthesis takes place here. Each leaf has tiny pores called **stomata,** through which it absorbs carbon dioxide. Plants also use a green substance called **chlorophyll** to absorb **solar energy**.

2 The water and minerals are transported up the **stem** through tubes called **xylem**.

4 The solar energy helps to **combine** the water, minerals and carbon dioxide. This reaction produces **glucose**, which the plant uses to grow. It also produces **oxygen**, which is released into the air.

Xylem are like the veins of the plant.

5 The glucose is transported around the plant through tubes called **phloem**.

Phloem are like the arteries of the plant.

1 The **roots** absorb **water** and **minerals** from the soil.

Plant respiration

It is not just animals that perform respiration – plants respire as well. **During the day**, plants take in carbon dioxide and some oxygen, and they also release the oxygen they don't need. **During the night**, plants cannot perform photosynthesis, so they take in the oxygen they need for respiration, and release carbon dioxide.

By the end of this lesson, you will know the recipe for photosynthesis.

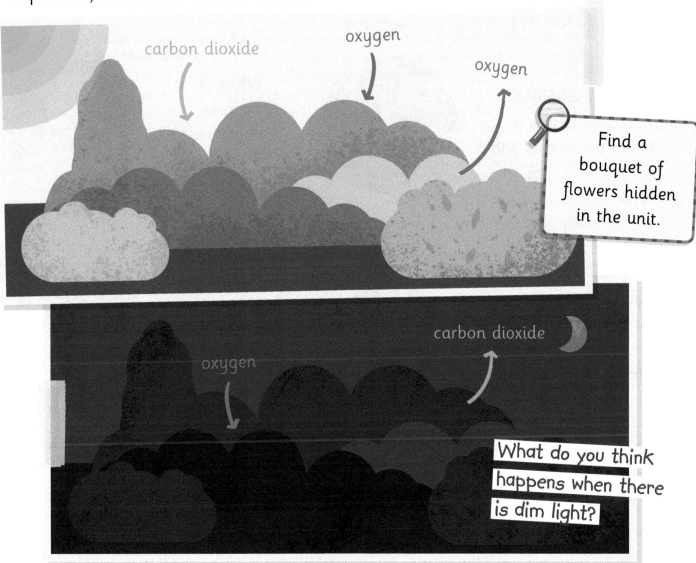

carbon dioxide

oxygen

oxygen

Find a bouquet of flowers hidden in the unit.

oxygen

carbon dioxide

What do you think happens when there is dim light?

Investigate STAGE 2

- In the same groups, revise the content on these two pages.
- Each group member comes up with a question for the quiz.
- On a new sheet of paper, each group member writes their question.

WHY IS PHOTOSYNTHESIS SO IMPORTANT?

Photosynthesis is one of the most important natural processes on Earth. Without plants, life as we know it on our planet would not be possible. Let's see why:

Food

Some of the **glucose** produced by plants is stored in their fruits and roots. When we eat apples, oranges, carrots and potatoes, we get **energy** and **nutrients**.

Oxygen

When plants perform photosynthesis, they produce oxygen, which all animals need to **stay alive**!

Global warming

Climate change is caused by global warming, which is caused by the release of **carbon dioxide** into the Earth's atmosphere. Who loves eating up carbon dioxide? That's right: plants! By planting more forests, we can help reduce global warming.

Habitats for animals

Plants provide food for other animals, and in many cases, they also provide a **home**. For example, the habitat of a squirrel is a tree, which is also the provider of its food.

Can you think of other uses that humans have for plants?

Investigate   STAGE 3

- In the same groups, revise the content on this page.
- Each group member comes up with a question for the quiz.
- On a new sheet of paper, each group member writes their question.
- Finally, revise the last five pages of this unit. Each group member writes another question. These questions are for the fourth round: the *bonus round*.

OBSERVING PLANT RESPIRATION

Hands On...

Before you start
During photosynthesis, plants release oxygen into the atmosphere.

Materials
freshly cut leaf, magnifying glass, sunlight, transparent bowl or glass, water

Method
1 Fill the glass or bowl with water.

2 Place the freshly cut leaf in the water.

3 Place the glass or bowl in a sunny area of your classroom.

4 Leave the leaf for about an hour.

5 Observe the leaf with a magnifying glass.

Conclusion
What has happened to the leaf?

What happens if you lightly shake the bowl or glass?

Repeat the experiment, but this time put one leaf in darkness and one in sunlight. Which leaf produced more oxygen?

1 🎧 **Listen and identify the correct box.**

1 What part of the plant does Elaine think is most important?

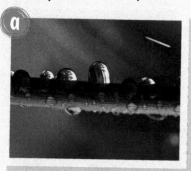 **a**    **b**    **c**

2 Which part of a flower does Jerry not know?

 **a**    **b**    **c**

3 What type of pollination does Elaine describe?

 **a**    **b**    **c**

2 **Complete the sentences with the correct forms of the words *can*, *be* or *do*.**

a Some plants reproduce asexually. This means fertilisation ..... take place.

b Plants ..... live without performing the process of photosynthesis.

c Some glucose ..... stored in fruits and vegetables. That is why we eat them.

d By planting more forests, we ..... help reduce the harmful effects of global warming.

e The glucose ..... transported around the plant through tubes called phloem.

f When the flower withers and dies, the seeds ..... dispersed.

1 Identify the types of asexual plants in the images.

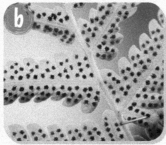

2 Look at the pictures. How are plants important for us in each case? Write full sentences in your notebook.

Investigate — FINALE

Assessment link
Go to page 84 for more activities.

- Each group takes it in turns to be quizmasters. The other groups take part in the quiz.
- There will be four rounds. Each round has five questions.
- When it is your group's turn, divide up the responsibilities:
  - One person reads out the questions.
  - One person corrects the answers.
  - One person times each round.
  - Two people hand out and collect sheets of paper for the answers.

5

WHICH FORCES ARE INVISIBLE?

Look and see...

Can you name the properties of these materials?

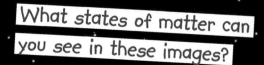
What states of matter can you see in these images?

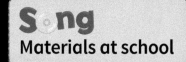
Song
Materials at school

What do you call the processes by which water changes from one state to another?

D▶CUMENTARY
Forces

Investigate

In this unit, you will make a materials classroom display. To do this, you will:

- learn more about matter, including the concepts of mass, volume and density.
- find out the volume of a solid object.
- identify the properties of certain materials.
- learn about contact and non-contact forces.
- discover why things float.

WHAT IS THE MATTER?

Everything in the Universe is made of **matter**. The chair you are sitting on, the book you are reading and even your body is made up of matter. Matter is anything that **occupies space** and **has mass**.

Mass

Mass is the **amount of matter** in an object. For example, a watermelon has a greater mass than an orange. We measure mass using weighing scales. Mass is measured in grams (g) and kilograms (kg).

How many grams are there in a Kilogram?

Volume

Volume is the **amount of space** an object occupies. For example, a golf ball has a greater volume than a marble. We can measure volume using a measuring jug. Volume is measured in millilitres (ml) and litres (l).

How many millilitres are there in a centilitre?

Can you think of an object that has a big volume but little mass?

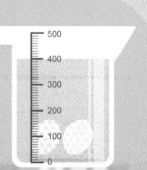

400 ml
- 300 ml
100 ml

Try this ...

Measuring the mass of a liquid

1 Place a glass or plastic container on a weighing scale.

2 Record the mass of the container.

3 Pour water into the container and record the new mass.

4 Calculate the mass of the liquid by subtracting the mass of the empty container from the mass of the full container.

Measuring the volume of solids

1 Fill a measuring jug with water up to the 300 ml mark.

2 Place an object into the water.

3 Write down the total volume of the water and the object.

4 Calculate the volume of the object by subtracting 300 from the total value.

States of matter

Matter occurs in **three different states**: solid, liquid and gas. Let's take a closer look at these properties of matter.

Matter is made up of very small particles, called **atoms**. When the **temperature** of matter decreases or increases, the atoms move closer together or further apart.

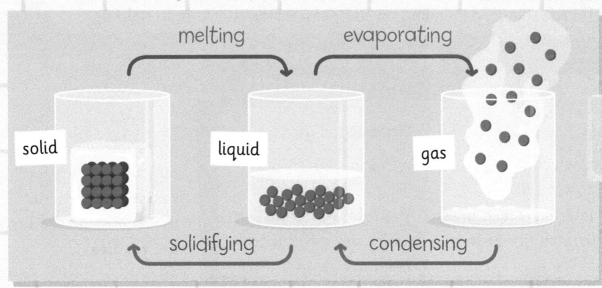

We can change the state of matter by **melting**, **evaporating**, **condensing** or **solidifying** it.

How are these things changing state?

Investigate   STAGE 1

- At home, save up some recyclable materials.
- Make sure you have at least one paper or cardboard object; one plastic object; one metal object; and one glass object.
- Clean them with water and soap, if necessary.

WHAT IS THE OPPOSITE OF FLEXIBLE?

If matter is the stuff from which everything is made, then what is a material? **Materials** are substances which are made up of matter. Materials can be made up of one type of matter or more than one type of matter. We use different materials to make different things, depending on the **properties** that a material has.

Properties of materials

Hardness

Materials which are difficult to scratch are **hard**. Materials which are easy to scratch are **soft**.

Diamonds are the hardest naturally occurring material on Earth.

Talc is a soft mineral because it is easy to scratch.

Flexibility

Materials which are easy to bend are **flexible**. Materials which are difficult to bend are **rigid**.

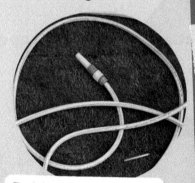

Rubber is a flexible material.

Wood is a rigid material.

Can you think of any other rigid or flexible materials?

Resistance

Materials which are difficult to break are **resistant**. Materials which are easy to break are **fragile**.

Plastic is a resistant material.

Glass is a fragile material.

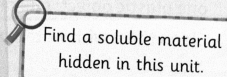

Find a soluble material hidden in this unit.

Thermal conduction

Materials which do not let heat travel through them easily are called **thermal insulators**. Materials which let heat travel through them easily are called **thermal conductors**.

The metal aluminium is a thermal conductor

Wood is a thermal insulator.

Elasticity

Materials which are easy to stretch are **elastic**. Materials which are not easy to stretch are **inelastic**.

Rubber is an elastic material.

Metal is an inelastic material.

Can you explain the difference between natural and manmade materials?

By the end of this lesson, you will be able to describe the properties of materials.

Solubility

If a material dissolves in a liquid, we say that it is **soluble**. If a material does not dissolve in a liquid, we say that it is **insoluble**.

Salt is a soluble material.

Rocks are insoluble materials.

Can you think of any other soluble or insoluble materials?

Investigate   STAGE 2

- Place your recyclable materials on a table.
- Find out about the properties of each material: hardness, flexibility, resistance, thermal conduction, elasticity and solubility.
- Record your findings on a sheet of A4 paper.
- You could make a table and write a tick or a cross for each material.

WHAT ARE CONTACT FORCES?

What happens when you kick a football in the playground? When you kick the ball, you apply a **force** to it. In this case, you are making the ball **move**. Before you kicked the ball, it was at **rest**. Forces can also change the **shape** of an object.

There are **two main types of forces**: contact forces and non-contact forces. **Contact forces** are forces that act[1] when we make contact with an object. Here are some examples.

Friction

Friction is a contact force that stops things moving or slows things down. For example, when you move your book across the desk, you have to make an effort. This is because there is a force of friction between the book and desk.

Try this ...

Check out this easy friction experiment.

1 Work with a partner.

2 Get two school books with the same number of pages – like the ones you're reading right now and put them side by side.

3 Open the book on the left on the back page and then open the book on the right on the first page and put it over the back page of the book on the left.

4 Continue putting the pages of the two books over each other.

5 When you have turned all the pages, try pulling the books apart.

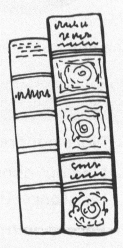

Is it easy to pull the books apart? What causes this?

Push and pull

When you push or pull a door, you make contact with it. The force you apply makes the door open.

Think about the things you push or pull every day. Make a list.

By the end of this lesson, you will know the difference between contact and non-contact forces.

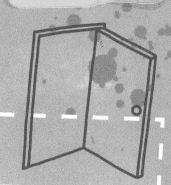

Changing shape

We can also change the shape of objects by applying force.

We can mould[2] clay into a shape by applying force with our hands. The clay **keeps the shape** we give it.

Some materials are elastic. When we apply force to them, their shape changes. But when we stop applying the force, they **return to their original state**.

Can you think of any other elastic objects?

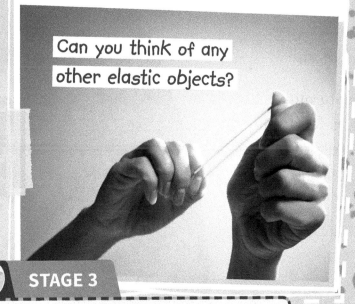

Investigate   STAGE 3

- **Test out the effect of contact forces on the materials.**
  - Try pushing your materials across a surface to test their friction.
  - Apply force to the materials to see if you can change their shape.
- **Record your findings on a separate sheet of paper.**

[1] **to act:** to do something
[2] **to mould:** to change the shape of something with your hands

61

WHAT ARE NON-CONTACT FORCES?

Non-contact forces are forces that do not require contact with an object. That is why non-contact forces are also called invisible forces. Let's look at two non-contact forces: **gravity** and **magnetism**.

Gravity

Gravity is a force that attracts objects towards each other. Any object that has **mass** exerts a force of gravity. The more mass it has, the stronger its force of gravity is. The Earth has so much mass that its force of gravity pulls everything **towards its centre**. That's why we are pulled down towards the ground!

Gravity makes the leaves fall from the tree to the ground in autumn.

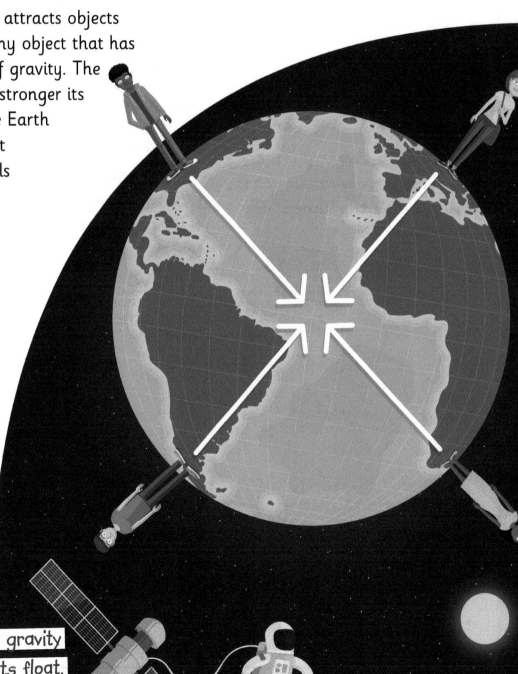

In space, the force of gravity is very weak, so objects float. This is why astronauts float.

Magnetism

Have you ever thought about why magnets stick to your fridge? A magnet is an object that produces a force called **magnetism**. This force can either **attract** or **repel**. Certain metals can have magnetic forces, for example iron, nickel and cobalt.

Magnets have **two poles**: a **south** pole and a **north** pole. If we put two magnets together:

By the end of this lesson, you will know why magnets stick to your fridge.

The north pole will attract the south pole.

The north pole will repel the other north pole, and so will the south poles.

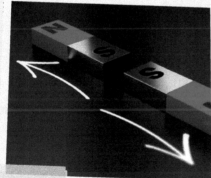

Try this ...

Check out this easy magnetism experiment.

1 Hold a paper clip in contact with a magnet.

2 Then attach another paper clip to the first one.

3 Continue attaching paper clips until you cannot attach any more.

How long was your paper clip chain? Compare with your classmates. What happens when you remove the magnet? Does the chain stay together?

Investigate — STAGE 4

- Test out the effect of non-contact forces on the materials.
- How does gravity affect the materials if you pick them up and let go of them? Do not test this out on glass!
- Using a magnet, check if any of the materials are affected by magnetism.
- Record your findings on a separate sheet of paper.

WHICH FORCE STOPS US FROM SINKING?

By the end of this lesson you will know how density makes something float or not.

Why does a heavy log float on the water, but a small stone sink? When you place an object in water, the **force of gravity** pushes the object to the bottom, but another force pushes the object upwards. We call this force **buoyancy**.

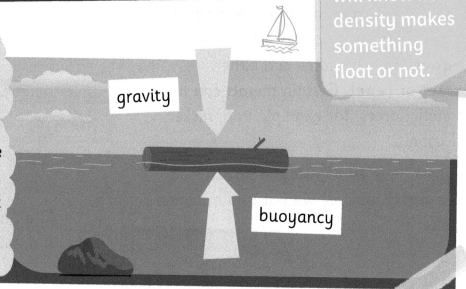

gravity

buoyancy

Whether an object sinks or floats in a liquid **depends on the material** it is made of.

If an object is light for its size, it floats. These objects have a **low density of matter**.

If an object is heavy for its size, it sinks. These objects have a **high density of matter**.

Do you float or sink in water?

Some objects are **light** for their size because they contain **air**. Large ships weigh a lot, but because their hull is hollow they are light for their size and have a low density.

 STAGE 5

- **Complete the experiment on page 65 using your materials from the previous stages.**
- **Record your findings on a separate sheet of paper.**

64

WILL IT SINK OR FLOAT?

Hands On...

Before we start
Depending on its density, an object will sink or float.

Materials
10 objects made of different materials (including your materials from this unit), tub of water

Method

1 Fill a tub with water.

2 Examine the 10 objects that you are going to put in the water.

3 Before putting them in the water, predict if they will sink or float.

4 Write down your predictions in a notebook.

5 Place each object in the water and observe.

6 Record your observations in the notebook.

Conclusion
How many objects sank and how many floated?

Were any of your predictions wrong? If so, why were they wrong?

Write down why you think each object sank or floated.

1 🎧 **Listen and identify the correct box.**

1 What material does Niall recycle the most?

 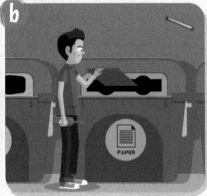 

2 How does Niall reduce the amount of plastic he uses?

3 What does Niall reuse at home?

2 **Complete the sentences in your notebook.**

a The window has ..... (break) because glass is a fragile material.

b The apple has .....(fall) off the tree because of the force of gravity.

c The stone has ..... (sink) to the bottom of the pond because it is dense.

d The magnet has .....(stick) to the fridge because it attracts metal.

1 Look at the materials. In your notebook, write sentences that describe the properties of each one. Use the words in the box to help you.

> thermal conductor   elastic   flexible   fragile
> hard   inelastic   insoluble   thermal insulator
> resistant   rigid   soft   soluble

2 Look at the pictures. What type of force does each one show?

Investigate   FINALE

- Bring your materials to class.
- Set up a display on your desk with your materials and your findings on the four sheets of paper.
- Walk around the classroom and observe your classmates' displays.

✓ Assessment link

Go to page 86 for more activities.

6

HOW HAVE MACHINES CHANGED THE WORLD?

Look and see...

What do you think life was like before these machines were invented?

Are these inventions important in your daily life?

DOCUMENTARY
Inventions that changed the world

Investigate

In this unit, you will carry out research into simple and complex machines in your home and your neighbourhood, and create a slide presentation. To do this, you will:

- learn more about simple and complex machines.
- understand that by applying effort to pulleys, inclined planes and levers, we can lift heavy objects more easily.
- distinguish between the different classes of levers.
- learn about the discoveries made by Archimedes, Newton and other innovators.

WHY ARE MACHINES SO IMPORTANT?

Machines **make our lives easier** because they help us to do work. There are **two main types** of machines: simple and complex. **Simple machines** have few or no moving parts. **Complex machines** have several[1] parts and contain simple machines. There are **six simple machines**: inclined plane, screw, pulley, wheel and axle, lever and wedge. We are going to look at three of them in detail: inclined planes, pulleys and levers.

We use inclined planes, pulleys and levers to move heavy loads. A **load** is the weight of an object. To move a load, we have to apply effort. **Effort** is the amount of force required to move the load.

> I have got to make a lot of effort to move this load!

HEAVY

Inclined plane

An inclined plane is a **tilted[2] surface** which goes **from a low point to a high point**. We use inclined planes to move a heavy load up and down. The smaller the incline, the easier it is to move an object up using an inclined plane.

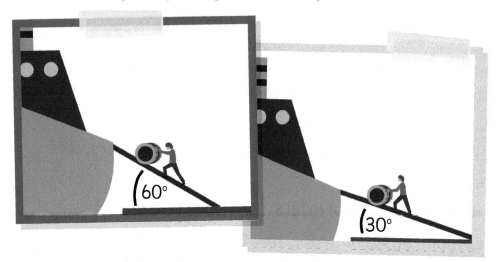

60°

30°

Another word for an inclined plane is a ramp. Are there any ramps in your school or in your community? Why are ramps important?

Pulley

A pulley is a simple machine which is made up of a **wheel and a rope or cable**. The wheel has a groove[3] in it and the rope goes around the wheel. When you **pull down on one end** of the rope **the other end goes up**. The wheel helps to move the load. We use pulleys to lift and lower heavy loads.

By the end of this lesson, you will know what a groove is.

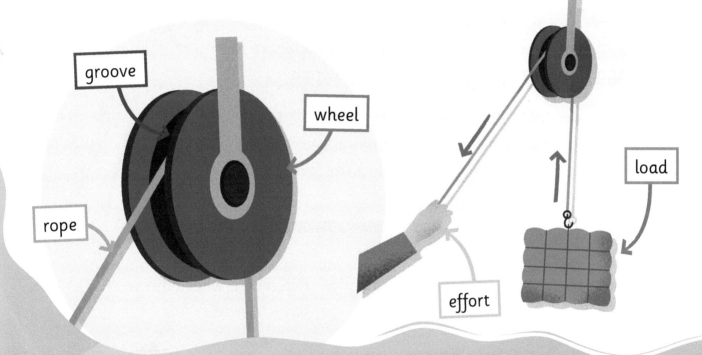

groove

wheel

rope

load

effort

What type of force is being applied to the rope?

Is it a contact or non-contact force?

Investigate STAGE 1

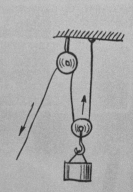

- On your way home from school, keep an eye out for any ramps and pulleys you can see.

- If possible, take photos of them.

- When you get home, record where you saw them and what they were being used for.

[3]**groove:** a long, narrow cut in a hard material
[2]**tilted:** not flat or horizontal
[1]**several:** more than one

WHERE ARE THE LEVERS ON YOUR BODY?

By the end of this lesson, you will know how many classes of levers there are.

A lever is made up of a **rigid bar** and a **fulcrum**. The rigid bar rests on the fulcrum. When we push down on one end of the rigid bar, the other end goes up. By pushing down, we are applying **effort**.

There are different **classes** of levers, depending on where the load and effort are located in relation to the fulcrum.

In a **class 1 lever**, the fulcrum is between the load and the effort.

Examples: see-saws, scissors, pliers, oar of a boat

Find a class 1 lever hidden somewhere in this unit.

In a **class 2 lever**, the load is between the effort and the fulcrum.

Examples: nutcracker, wheelbarrow, bottle opener

In a **class 3 lever**, the effort is between the fulcrum and the load.

Examples: stapler, tongs, tweezers

Investigate STAGE 2

- Search your home for different examples of levers.
- Decide if they are class 1, 2 or 3 levers.
- Write down your findings.
- Take photos of the levers, if possible.

When was the last time you used a lever? What class was it?

MAKE YOUR OWN LEVER

Hands On...

Before you start
Depending on where the fulcrum is in a lever, we have to apply more or less force.

Materials
lots of similar small objects (rubbers, clips…), pencil, plasticine, two plastic cups, ruler (30 cm)

Method
1 Set up a class 1 lever. The pencil will act as the fulcrum.

2 Stick a plastic cup to each end of the ruler with plasticine.

3 Put some objects in one cup. This is the load.

4 Place the fulcrum at the 5 cm mark. Predict how many objects you will have to put in the other cup to lift the load.

5 Test your hypothesis by adding objects one by one.

6 Repeat with the fulcrum at these marks: 10 cm, 15 cm, 20 cm.

7 Record your findings in your notebook.

Conclusions
How many objects did you need to lift the load at each point?

Did you need to add more or fewer objects as the fulcrum moved away from the load?

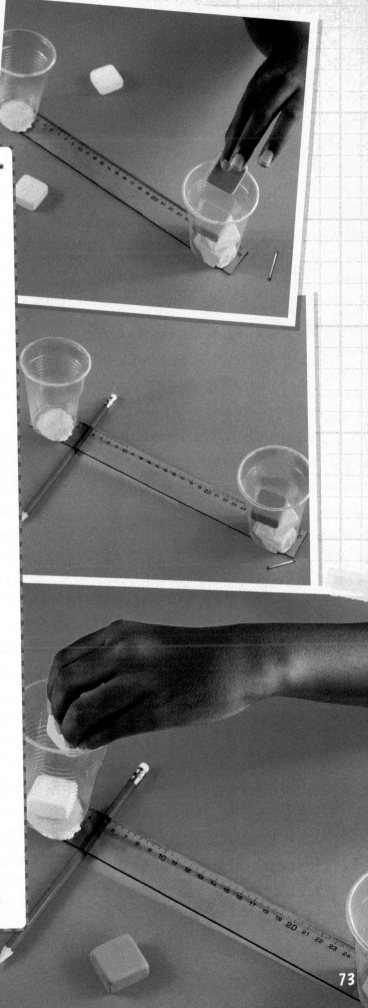

WHAT INVENTIONS DO YOU USE EVERY DAY?

Advances in science are made by great thinkers and inventors, like **Archimedes** and **Isaac Newton.**

Archimedes

Archimedes was an Ancient Greek mathematician, engineer, inventor and astronomer. He lived in Syracuse more than 2,000 years ago.

An **Archimedes' screw** is made up of a screw inside a hollow[1] pipe. This machine is used to transfer water from low-lying areas to higher areas. The screw inside the pipe was turned around by hand using a crank or by a windmill.

Find out who Archimedes worked for.

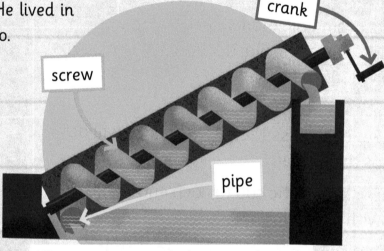

crank

screw

pipe

Water is taken in at the bottom and travels up the threads[2] of the screw as it rotates.

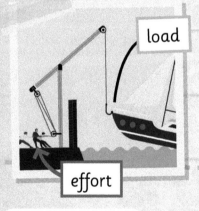

load

effort

Archimedes developed a weapon called the **Archimedes' Claw** to defend the city of Syracuse from Roman invaders. The Claw was similar to a crane and had a hook that could lift an attacking ship upwards. This would cause the ship to sink or capsize[3].

Isaac Newton

Isaac Newton was an English mathematician, astronomer and physicist. He was born in 1643. He is best known for his discovery of the three **laws of motion** and the **law of gravity**, the invisible force that controls how everything in the Universe moves.

After observing an apple fall from a tree, Newton realised that gravity is a **pulling force**.

The discoveries of Archimedes and Newton helped the progress of mankind. Let's look at some other inventions which had a big impact on the way people lived.

3500 BC

Before the invention of **the wheel**, people had to push or pull loads along the ground.

200 BC

The compass was invented in China around 2,000 years ago. Before it was invented, navigators had to use landmarks to find their way.

AD 1879

The **light bulb** was invented by the American inventor Thomas Edison. Before its invention, people had to use oil lamps or candles to illuminate their homes.

AD 1903

The **aeroplane** was invented by the Wright Brothers. Air travel changed the way people travelled because it made long journeys quicker and easier.

AD 1974

The **personal computer** was the first computer that people had in their homes. It allowed people to prepare documents, make calculations, play games and later use the internet.

Find out the first names of the Wright Brothers. Who made the first flight?

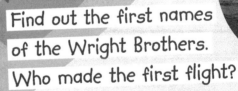

Look back

What force makes compasses work?

Investigate STAGE 3

- Search your home for examples of the inventions on this page.
- Make a list and take photos, if possible.

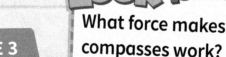

[1] **hollow:** with an empty space inside
[2] **thread:** the inclined plane that goes around a screw
[3] **to capsize:** to turn upside-down in the water

1 **Read the diary and write the missing words in your notebook.**

Example Today has been so much fun! I went on a school trip to a car
   a factory. I have always wondered how cars ..... made, so I was very
   b excited to finally find out. One of the workers from the factory .....
      us a tour of the factory floor. He explained that cars are complex
      machines, although they contain simple machines. Cars can
   c move easily along the ground ..... they have four wheels and two
   d axles. To get into a car, you ..... to pull on the door handle, which is
      a lever. The workers connect the car parts together using screws,
   e ..... are simple machines as well. Sometimes the workers need to
      work underneath the car. To do this, they lift the car up using a
   f screw. ..... the car is finished, it leaves the factory by going down a
      ramp, which is an inclined plane.

2 **Put the verbs into the past continuous. Copy and complete the sentences in your notebook.**
   a Isaac Newton ..... (sit) under an apple tree when an apple fell on his head.
   b Archimedes ..... (take) a bath when he made an important discovery.
   c Wilbur Wright ..... (run) next to the plane when his brother made the
      first flight.
   d Archimedes was killed by a Roman soldier when he ..... (work) on a
      mathematical problem.

1. Look at the pictures. In your notebook, write down which class of lever you see in each one.

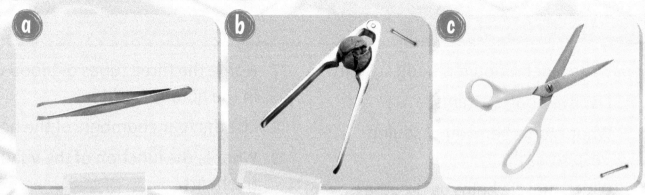

2. In your notebook, make a timeline of these inventions.

3. Write the names of these inventions in your notebook.

Investigate · FINALE

- Create a slide presentation with all the information you collected in stages 1–3.
- Prepare separate slides for the ramps and pulleys you saw.
- Prepare separate slides for the different classes of levers.
- Include a slide about one of the inventions you found at home.
- Practise your presentation with a partner and then present it to the rest of the class.

Assessment link

Go to page 88 for more activities.

1 Questions

Think about it

1 Write a definition for 'body system'.

2 List five body systems.

3 What is another way of saying 'respiration'?

4 Which muscle helps us breathe?

5 What are the alveoli covered in?

6 What do we call the amount of air we can fit in our lungs?

7 Name the three types of blood vessels in the human body.

8 List the four chambers of the heart.

9 What is the function of the valves in the heart?

10 What is the circulatory system?

Think harder

1 What is another name for 'body system'? Why do we call it that?

2 List three vital signs.

3 Describe the process of respiration.

4 Describe what happens to oxygen and carbon dioxide in the alveoli.

5 How can you and a classmate measure your lung capacities?

6 Explain how the three types of blood vessels work?

7 Which lung is smaller than the other? Why?

8 What do the respiratory system and the circulatory system have in common?

9 True or false: Our blood cannot carry oxygen and carbon dioxide at the same time.

10 What happens if our heart stops pumping?

Study aid

Tip

One of the best ways to learn about a subject is to research it and create a **presentation**. You can make a presentation about any topic and you can present it to your class, your friends or your family. To make it clear and attractive, use a slide presentation program on a computer.

HOW TO KEEP HEALTHY

DO LOTS OF EXERCISE. **ONE GOOD ACTIVITY** IS GYMNASTICS.

Create a title slide for your presentation. Include a picture if you want.

Do not include too much text on each slide. People will spend too much time reading and not listening to you.

Include pictures to make your presentation more interesting to look at.

Make cue cards to help you remember what you are going to say. And practise with them!

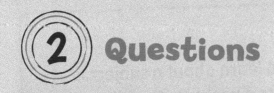

2 Questions

Think about it

1 List three symptoms of the common cold.

2 What body system does the flu affect?

3 Why is it best to stay at home if you catch chicken pox?

4 What is first aid?

5 List five nutrients we need to get from the food we eat.

6 Why is fast food bad for you?

7 How many hours of sleep do you need each night?

8 Explain three things you should do to take care of your personal hygiene.

9 What instrument do doctors use to measure your blood pressure?

10 How can smoking negatively affect your health?

Think harder

1 Identify two differences between a cold and the flu.

2 Why is it not good to scratch your skin when you have chicken pox?

3 How do we get common illnesses?

4 Apart from asthma, what other illnesses require people to take medicine every day? Find out.

5 What should you do if you have a cold?

6 What should we do before giving first aid?

7 If someone has an accident at school, what is the first thing you should do?

8 Name two things exercise is good for.

9 How many hours a day do you spend looking at screens? Is it too much or is it OK?

10 Why should we limit our screen time?

Study aid

Tip

You may often come across words you do not understand. Sometimes you see a word and think: 'I have seen that word before, but I cannot remember what it means!' One easy way to help you remember these difficult words is to make a **vocabulary notebook**. You write the word on the left-hand side of the page and the meaning of the word next to it. You can include the word in your own language, too!

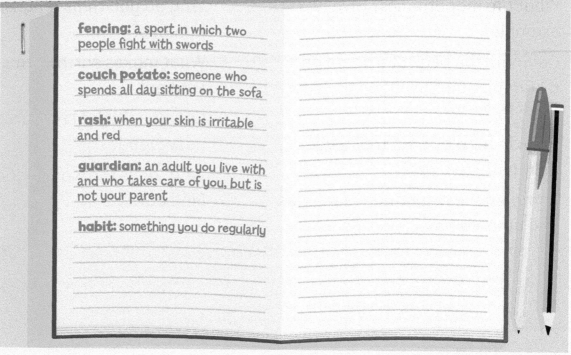

fencing: a sport in which two people fight with swords

couch potato: someone who spends all day sitting on the sofa

rash: when your skin is irritable and red

guardian: an adult you live with and who takes care of you, but is not your parent

habit: something you do regularly

3 Questions

Think about it

1 Name the three different types of nutrition.

2 Write definitions for *viviparous* and *oviparous*.

3 Write down three examples of carnivorous mammals.

4 What type of beak do hawks and toucans have?

5 Where do reptiles lay their eggs?

6 Name three invertebrates that amphibians eat.

7 What type of nutrition do the majority of fish perform?

8 What percentage of all animal species on Earth are invertebrates?

9 Name two subgroups for each of these groups: arthropods and molluscs.

10 What invertebrate group do sea anemones belong to?

Think harder

1 Are llamas herbivores, omnivores or carnivores?

2 What are monotremes? Give two examples.

3 Compare the beak of a heron and a hummingbird. What do they use them for?

4 How do reptiles treat their eggs differently to birds?

5 Compare the respiration of reptiles and amphibians.

6 Explain the process of metamorphosis to a partner.

7 Why do you think jellyfish sting humans?

8 What makes earthworms shiny? Find out.

9 Can you think of two bivalves we eat as seafood?

10 What does the word *arthropod* mean? Find out.

Study aid

Invertebrates
- Arthropods
  - Insects
    - Bees
    - Ants
    - Butterflies
  - Arachnids
    - Spiders
    - Scorpions
  - Crustaceans
    - Crabs
    - Lobsters
    - Shrimp
  - Myriapods
    - Centipedes
    - Millipedes
- Molluscs
  - Gastropods
    - Snails
    - Slugs
  - Cephalopods
    - Squid
    - Octopuses
  - Bivalves
    - Oysters
    - Clams
- Annelids
  - Worms
- Echinoderms
  - Starfish
  - Urchins
  - Sea cucumbers
- Cnidarians
  - Jellyfish
  - Sea anemones
- Poriferans
  - Sponges

Tip

Concept maps are a useful way of organising information so that it is easier to remember. For example, you can make a concept map of the different invertebrate groups you learnt about in Unit 3. Why don't you draw pictures to make your concept map more fun to look at?

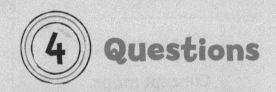

④ Questions

Think about it

1 What are the names of the male and female parts of a flower?

2 What attracts animals to the flowers of plants?

3 What are the female plant cells called?

4 Name three types of plants that reproduce asexually.

5 What is the name of the process by which plants make their own food?

6 What are the functions of the roots and stem?

7 Why can't plants perform photosynthesis at night?

8 What is the function of chlorophyll?

9 Give three reasons why plants are important.

10 What causes global warming?

Think harder

1 Explain the function of each part of the pistil.

2 Explain the process of animal pollination to a partner.

3 How are stolons and rhizomes different?

4 Find out more examples of stolons and rhizomes.

5 Write a definition of the word *autotroph*.

6 Describe the function of the leaves in photosynthesis.

7 How are veins and arteries similar to some parts of a plant?

8 Describe the process of plant respiration to a partner.

9 What can we do to prevent global warming?

10 Trees give squirrels two things. What are they?

Study aid

DAY

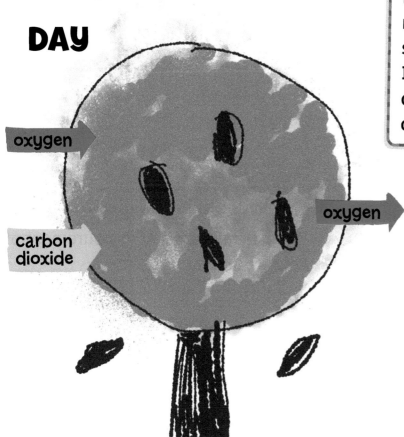

Tip

Drawing **diagrams** can help you remember the different parts of something you are learning about. It can also help you to understand a process. Why don't you draw a diagram of something from Unit 4?

NIGHT

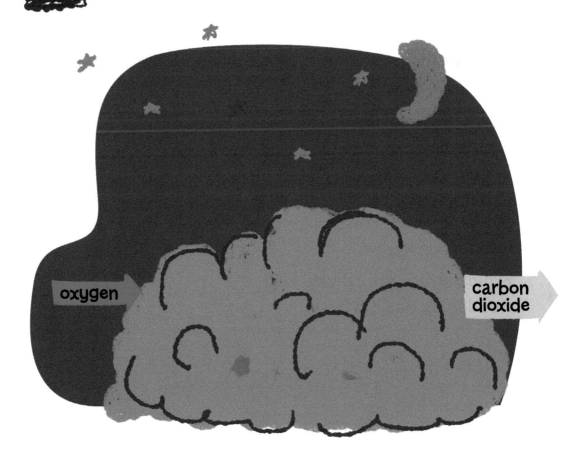

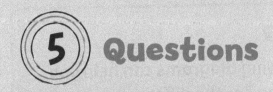

Questions

Think about it

1 What is everything in the Universe made of?

2 Write definitions for the terms *mass* and *matter*.

3 What tools do we use to measure mass and volume?

4 What are the very small particles that make up matter called?

5 What are the three states of matter?

6 What property do materials that are easy to scratch have?

7 Write two examples of resistant materials.

8 Which type of force is gravity?

9 What are the units of measurement of volume and matter?

10 What do we call the force that pushes an object in water up?

Think harder

1 Write the method for measuring the mass of a liquid.

2 Write the method for measuring the volume of a solid.

3 Draw a diagram that shows the arrangement of atoms in solids, liquids and gases.

4 Write two examples of soluble materials and two examples of insoluble materials.

5 Explain why we use plastic and wooden cooking tools.

6 Write an example of the force of friction.

7 Describe to a partner what happens when we put two magnets together.

8 What is the difference between flexible materials and elastic materials?

9 Can you think of a way to help you float in water?

10 How does air affect whether an object floats or sinks?

Study aid

MATTER

Tip

Sometimes, the new concepts we learn are difficult to remember, especially when we are studying concepts related to physics, such as magnetism and gravity. So, it is a good idea to make **definition cards** to help you understand and revise difficult terms and their meanings.

Substances which are made up of matter; can be made up of one type of matter or more than one type of matter.

FRICTION

Forces that act when we make contact with an object.

GRAVITY

SOLUBLE

The amount of space an object occupies.

Forces that do not require contact with an object.

6 Questions

Think about it

1 Write definitions for the terms *simple machine* and *complex machine*.

2 What do we have to apply to move a load?

3 Explain what we use inclined planes for.

4 Name the parts of a pulley.

5 Where is the load in a class 2 lever?

6 Where and when did Archimedes live?

7 Name two inventions of Archimedes.

8 What did Isaac Newton discover?

9 Who invented the light bulb?

10 What do we use personal computers for?

Think harder

1 Do all complex machines need electrical energy to work?

2 What do inclined planes, pulleys and levers have in common?

3 Is it easier to push a load up an inclined plane with an incline of 30° or 50°? Explain why.

4 What is the purpose of the groove on the wheel of a pulley?

5 What makes one class of lever different from another?

6 Are there any levers on your body?

7 Explain to a partner how Archimedes' screw works.

8 Isaac Newton also improved the telescope. Find out how.

9 In your own words, tell a partner how the invention of the wheel changed people's lives.

10 Which invention do you think was more important: the aeroplane or the light bulb?

Study aid

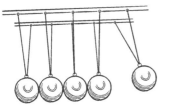

Tip

When you have to read a long text, it is sometimes hard to keep all the information in your head! Like some foods, long texts can be hard to digest and it can be difficult to get the main ideas (nutrients) from them. One way of resolving this problem is to **highlight** or underline the key concepts in a text.

Isaac Newton was a scientist, astronomer and mathematician. He was born on 4 January 1647 in Lincolnshire, a county in England. He is considered to be one of the most important scientists of all time. Newton made many innovations during his life. He developed a law of gravity, which is one of the most important discoveries in the history of science. He also developed three laws of motion. 'Motion' is another word for 'movement'.

The first of these laws is the law of motion which says that an object that is at rest will continue to be at rest until a force acts upon it. The first law also says that any object that is in motion will continue to move in the same direction and at the same speed unless a force acts on it.

The second law of motion says that the greater the mass of an object, the greater the force needed to accelerate the object.

The third law is a very famous one. It says that for every action there is an equal and opposite reaction.

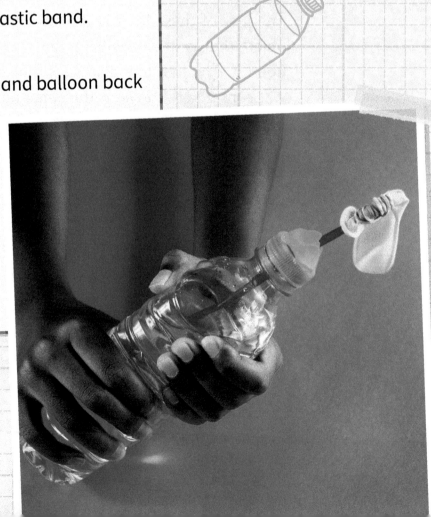

Before you start
The heart is the pump of the circulatory system. The veins, arteries and capillaries are the blood vessels through which the blood is transported.

Materials
plastic bottle, hammer, nail, straw, plasticine, balloon, elastic band, water

Method

1 With the help of an adult, make a hole in the bottle cap with the hammer and nail.

2 Pass the straw through the hole and seal with plasticine.

3 Put the balloon on the other end of the straw and seal using the elastic band.

4 Fill the bottle with water.

5 Put the cap with the straw and balloon back on the bottle.

6 Squeeze the bottle and observe what happens.

Conclusions
What part of the model represents the heart?

What do the water and straw represent?

Before you start

During emergencies, it is sometimes recommended that we put the injured person in the recovery position. This position keeps their airways open and allows them to breathe. The recovery position is used for people who are unresponsive but are still breathing.

Materials

a partner

Method

1 Get into pairs: one of you will be the injured person and the other will give first aid.

2 Open the injured person's mouth and tilt their head back.

3 Look, listen and feel to see if they are breathing. If they are breathing, put them in the recovery position.

4 Put their lower left arm pointing upwards.

5 Bring the other arm across their chest and put the hand against their left cheek.

6 Pull on their right knee and roll them on to their side.

Conclusions

Ask your partner if they are comfortable.

How did you check their breathing?

In a real-life situation, what would you do next?

③ More hands on...

Before you start
Magnifying glasses help us view arthropods up close. By closely observing them, we can see the different characteristics that help us classify them.

Materials
inexpensive magnifying glass, ruler, scissors, transparent plastic cup, transparent sticky tape

Method

1 With the help of an adult, remove the lens from the magnifying glass.

2 Test the lens to see from what distance you can clearly see an object. Use the ruler to measure the distance.

3 Then measure the plastic cup. Use the distance from step 2 and cut off the bottom of the cup.

4 Attach the lens to the cup with sticky tape.

5 Go out to the playground or a green space near your home, and look for arthropods to observe.

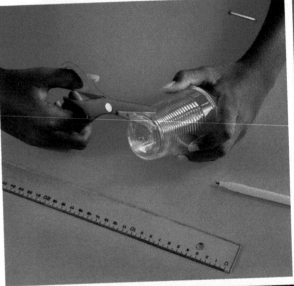

6 Write your findings in a notebook.

Conclusions
Which arthropods did you discover?

What characteristics distinguished them?

Make sure to release the bugs when you have finished observing them!

4 More hands on...

Before you start

Plants need sunlight to be able to perform photosynthesis. In order to obtain as much sunlight as possible, some plants grow towards the source of sunlight.

Materials

two plant pots, soil, pencil, seeds, water

Method

1 Fill the two pots with soil.

2 Make small holes in the soil with a pencil.

3 Place seeds in the holes and cover them with soil.

4 Water both pots.

5 Place one pot next to a window which receives a lot of light.

6 Place the other pot in a shadier part of the room.

7 Water regularly and observe what happens to the seedlings.

Conclusions

What happened to the seeds that were close to a strong source of light?

What happened to the seeds in the other pot?

Do you notice any other differences between the two pots? Explain your observation.

The plant's attraction to light is called *phototropism*.

5 More hands on...

Before you start

An object that is at rest stays at rest until a force acts on it. This is called *inertia*.

Materials

four heavy paper cups, A4 paper

Method

1 Work in groups of three.

2 Place one cup face-down on the table.

3 Place another cup on top of the first cup with a piece of paper in between.

4 Do the same with the next two cups until you have a tower of four cups.

5 Quickly pull out the top piece of paper.

6 Continue with the other two pieces of paper.

Conclusions

What happened to the cups?

Do you think you need to pull the paper out quickly?

Which forces make the cups fall down.

Are the cups affected by the force you apply when pulling the paper?

Find out who developed this law of inertia during the 17th century.

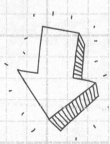

6 More hands on...

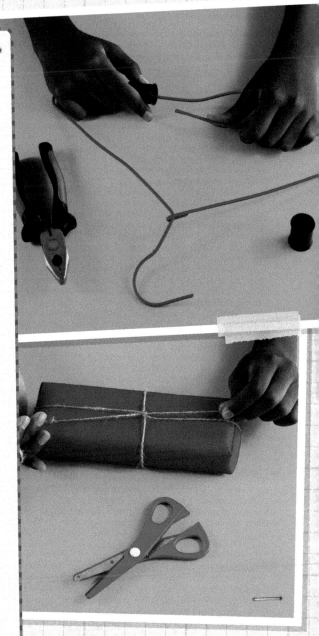

Before you start

Pulleys are made up of a wheel and a rope or cable. We use them to lift and lower heavy objects.

Materials

empty thread spool, heavy rectangular object, string, wire clothes hanger, wire cutter

Method

1 Work in pairs. Cut the bottom of the clothes hanger using the wire cutter.

2 Attach the empty thread spool by passing the open ends of the hanger through the hole in the spool.

3 Bend the ends of the hanger down so the spool does not detach from the hanger.

4 One pupil holds the hanger while the other ties the string around the object.

5 Pass the string over the spool.

6 Pull down on the string.

Conclusions

What happened when you pulled down on the string?

Can you think of any ways to improve your pulley? What is missing on the wheel?

Where are the load and the effort?

CAMBRIDGE
UNIVERSITY PRESS

Acknowledgements

The authors and publishers acknowledge the following sources of copyright material and are grateful for the permissions granted. While every effort has been made, it has not always been possible to identify the sources of all the material used, or to trace all copyright holders. If any omissions are brought to our notice, we will be happy to include the appropriate acknowledgements on reprinting and in the next update to the digital edition, as applicable.

Key: Unit = U, EM: End Matter

Photo acknowledgements

All the photographs are sourced from Getty Images.

U0: Ariel Skelley/DigitalVision; Laurence Monneret/Photographer's Choice; Pierre-Yves Babelon/Moment; Hero Images; fstop123/E+; FatCamera/E+; PeopleImages/E+; **U1:** Hero Images; fstop123/E+; Hill Street Studios/Blend Images; Westend61; krisanapong detraphiphat/Moment; BSIP/Universal Images Group; Jose Luis Pelaez Inc/Digitalvision; BSIP/Universal Images Group; Ian Hooton/Science Photo Library; kimberrywood/DigitalVision Vectors; ZenShui/Ale Ventura/PhotoAlto Agency RF Collections; Kreatiw/iStock/Getty Images Plus; SCIEPRO/Science Photo Library; SPRINGER MEDIZIN/Science Photo Library; Image Source; **U2:** Media for Medical/ Universal Images Group; Robert Niedring/MITO images; vitapix/iStock/Getty Images Plus; LittleBee80/iStock/Getty Images Plus; Blend Images - JGI/Jamie Grill; JGI/Jamie Grill; Kinzie Riehm/Image Source; ImagesBazaar; Tetra Images; Adrian Pope/ Photographer's Choice; Tuomas Lehtinen/Moment Open; puruan/iStock/Getty Images Plus; Baksiabat/iStock/Getty Images Plus; Seb Oliver/Cultura; gbh007/iStock/Getty Images Plus; fcafotodigital/E+; The Washington Post; Tim Graham/Getty Images News; Andy Crawford/Dorling Kindersley/Getty Images Plus; Vladimir Gerdo/TASS; Mikael Vaisanen/Corbis; Mikael Vaisanen/Corbis; Hero Images; KidStock/Blend Images; Natasha_Pankina/iStock/Getty Images Plus; KidStock/Blend Images; Natasha_ Pankina/iStock/Getty Images Plus; FG Trade/E+; ourlifelooklikeballoon/iStock/Getty Images Plus; Ute Grabowsky/Photothek; cristinairanzo/Moment; Amy Stocklein Images/Moment; Peter Dazeley/Photographer's Choice/Getty Images Plus; Compassionate Eye Foundation/DigitalVision; JGI/Jamie Grill; Floresco Productions/ Cultura; FrankRamspott/DigitalVision Vectors; LEOcrafts/DigitalVision Vectors; sam_ ding/DigitalVision Vectors; mightyisland/DigitalVision Vectors; J-Elgaard/E+; Ryan McVay/DigitalVision; svetikd/E+; Dorling Kindersley; owattaphotos/iStock/Getty Images Plus; Carsten Schanter/EyeEm; Seb Oliver/Cultura; Orbon Alija/E+; **U3:** Feng Wei Photography/Moment; Dan Mihai/Moment; edurivero/iStock/Getty Images Plus; MikeLane45/iStock/Getty Images Plus; Alexander Safonov/Moment; johnandersonphoto/iStock/Getty Images Plus; Daniela Duncan/Moment; Bob Stefko/ DigitalVision; Yi Fan Chin/EyeEm; mkurtbas/iStock/Getty Images Plus; Peter J Bardsley/ Moment Open; nameinfame/iStock/Getty Images Plus; Linda Pitkin/Nature Picture Library/Nature Picture Library; B&M Noskowski/E+; Reinhard Dirscherl/WaterFrame; Dorling Kindersley; Brian Mckay Photographyy/Moment; David Martin/Moment; Louise Heusinkveld/Oxford Scientific; Faba-Photograhpy/Moment; John Giustina/The Image Bank; Westend61; James Hager/robertharding; Francisco Rama/EyeEm; Kevin Elsby/ Corbis Documentary; Tier Und Naturfotografie J und C Sohns/Photographer's Choice; GooseFrol/iStock/Getty Images Plus; Cnuisin/iStock/Getty Images Plus; ElementalImaging/E+; Ger Bosma/Moment; Wilfried Martin; KenCanning/iStock/Getty Images Plus; Vismar Ravagnani/Moment; Arto Hakola/Moment; Rolf Muller/ imageBROKER; cotuvokne/iStock/Getty Images Plus; JohnWNixon/iStock/Getty Images Plus; Shaen Adey/Gallo Images; Omaly Darcia/iStock/Getty Images Plus; hchjjl/iStock/ Getty Images Plus; Buddy Mays/Corbis; carlacdesign/iStock/Getty Images Plus; Ken Kiefer 2/Cultura; Mint Images RF; FLPA/Colin Marshall/Corbis Documentary; LokFung/ DigitalVision Vectors; Bodo Schieren; vovashevchuk/iStock/Getty Images Plus; Nosyrevy/iStock/Getty Images Plus; Don Farrall/DigitalVision; carlacdesign/iStock/ Getty Images Plus; Shubham Sable/EyeEm; moodboard/Cultura; scubaluna/iStock/ Getty Images Plus; Gail Shotlander/Moment; Jane Burton/Dorling Kindersley carlacdesign/iStock/Getty Images Plus; ; TorriPhoto/Moment; Joao Inacio/Moment; Mint Images - Paul Edmondson/Mint Images RF; Philippe Marion/Moment; johnandersonphoto/iStock/Getty Images Plus; Vasilyevalara/iStock/Getty Images Plus; AllNikArt/iStock/Getty Images Plus; Tambako the Jaguar/Moment; Tom Creighton/ EyeEm; Mint Images - Frans Lanting; Colin Varndell/Photolibrary; © Santiago Urquijo/ Moment; Yiming Chen/Moment; ©Christopher Seufert Photography/Moment; Alex Bramwell/Moment; Will Heap/Dorling Kindersley; Daniela Duncan/Moment; Gerard Soury/Oxford Scientific; **U4:** undefined undefined/iStock/Getty Images Plus; Flavia Morlachetti/Moment; Manuel Breva Colmeiro/Moment; Jasmina007/E+; Antonia Adelmann/EyeEm; Ian.CuiYi/Moment; Chris Winsor/Moment; ONYXprj/iStock/Getty Images Plus; Ed Reschke/Photolibrary; P. Bonduel/Photolibrary; Gavin Kingcome Photography/Taxi; Nystudio/iStock/Getty Images Plus; James Darell/Cultura; Stella; KidStock/Blend Images; Sandra Standbridge/Moment; tom-iurchenko/iStock/Getty Images Plus; Katherine Jackson/EyeEm; tom-iurchenko/iStock/Getty Images Plus; Simon Gakhar/Moment; Simon Gakhar/Moment; Kristin Lee/Tetra images; Ed Reschke/ Photolibrary; Nuno Filipe Pereira/EyeEm; Peerawut Kesorncharoen/EyeEm; Barbara Rich/Moment; ElementalImaging/E+; BrianAJackson/iStock/Getty Images Plus; Manuel Breva Colmeiro/Moment; P. Bonduel/Photolibrary; tonaquatic/iStock/Getty Images Plus; Gavin Kingcome Photography/Taxi; Ed Reschke/Photolibrary; Merethe Svarstad Eeg/EyeEm; Pierdelune/iStock/Getty Images Plus; StockPlanets/iStock/Getty Images Plus; klebercordeiro/iStock/Getty Images Plus; fstop123/E+; **U5:** Xinzheng/Moment; David Franklin/Photographer's Choice RF; Ian O'Leary/Dorling Kindersley; taesmileland/iStock/Getty Images Plus; Devonyu/iStock/Getty Images Plus; 3DSculptor/iStock/Getty Images Plus; Valentino Nobile/EyeEm; Jose A. Bernat Bacete/ Moment Open; Toa55/iStock/Getty Images Plus; DonNichols/iStock/Getty Images Plus; Clive Streeter/Dorling Kindersley; jamtoons/DigitalVision Vectors; Eric Raptosh Photography; RyersonClark/E+; Don Klumpp/Stone; golfbress/iStock/Getty Images Plus; Magnilion/DigitalVision Vectors; Andrew Brookes/Cultura; De Agostini Picture Library; Kryssia Campos/Moment; Katja Kircher/Maskot; daizuoxin/iStock/Getty Images Plus; SEInnovation/iStock/Getty Images Plus; AllNikArt/iStock/Getty Images Plus; Natasha_Pankina/iStock/Getty Images Plus; ozgurdonmaz/iStock/Getty Images Plus; Vladimir Godnik/fStop; Steve Debenport/E+; mtv2020/iStock/Getty Images Plus; ; Foodcollection RF; Ailime/iStock/Getty Images Plus; ourlifelooklikeballoon/iStock/ Getty Images Plus; Alistair Berg/DigitalVision; Mint Images RF; ONYXprj/iStock/Getty Images Plus; cometary/E+; RunPhoto/DigitalVision; owattaphotos/iStock/Getty Images Plus; borchee/E+; pseudodaemon/DigitalVision Vectors; olm26250/iStock/Getty Images Plus; olm26250/iStock/Getty Images Plus; Ilona Shorokhova/iStock/Getty Images Plus; hchjjl/iStock/Getty Images Plus; ulimi/DigitalVision Vectors; filipfoto/iStock/Getty Images Plus; Ultra.F/Digitalvision; Julian Popov/EyeEm; VadimZakirov/iStock/Getty Images Plus; artisteer/iStock/Getty Images Plus; miwa_in_oz/iStock/Getty Images Plus; benimage/iStock/Getty Images Plus; Picsfive/iStock/Getty Images Plus; sikhorn/ iStock/Getty Images Plus; Toshiro Shimada/Moment; Jetta Productions/Dana Neely/ Juampiter/Moment; Andy Crawford/Dorling Kindersley; Dave & Les Jacobs/Blend Images; filipfoto/iStock/Getty Images Plus; **U6:** Bjarte Rettedal/DigitalVision; heshphoto/Image Source; Hakan Jansson/Maskot; Caiaimage/Chris Ryan; JGI/Jamie Grill/Tetra images; Busakorn Pongparnit/Moment; nuwatphoto/iStock/Getty Images Plus; Natasha_Pankina/iStock/Getty Images Plus; polygraphus/iStock/Getty Images Plus; Donal Husni/EyeEm; AnthonyRosenberg/iStock/Getty Images Plus; Yoyochow23/ iStock/Getty Images Plus; MarinaMariya/iStock/Getty Images Plus; jamtoons/ DigitalVision Vectors; ourlifelooklikeballoon/iStock/Getty Images Plus; setory/iStock/ Getty Images Plus; frimages/iStock/Getty Images Plus; LokFung/DigitalVision Vectors; ourlifelooklikeballoon/iStock/Getty Images Plus; jamtoons/DigitalVision Vectors; setory/iStock/Getty Images Plus, frimages/iStock/Getty Images Plus; Tetra Images; richcano/iStock/Getty Images Plus; oatawa/iStock/Getty Images Plus; Bettmann; Mark Madeo/Future Publishing tsirik/iStock/Getty Images Plus; Manuel Breva Colmeiro/ Moment; Will Heap/Dorling Kindersley; Kevin Summers/Photographer's Choice; Steve Gorton/Dorling Kindersley; AdamLukas/iStock/Getty Images Plus; Dorling Kindersley; Mario Gutiérrez/Moment; Science Photo Library; phive2015/iStock/Getty Images Plus; Dorling Kindersley; Will Heap/Dorling Kindersley; **EM:** PeopleImages/E+; neapneap/ iStock/Getty Images Plus; Vectorovich/iStock/Getty Images Plus; Agaten/iStock/Getty Images Plus; owattaphotos/iStock/Getty Images Plus; sezgen/iStock/Getty Images Plus; lemonadeserenade/iStock/Getty Images Plus; Nadydy/iStock/Getty Images Plus; lineartestpilot/iStock/Getty Images Plus;

Front cover photography by Richard Green/The Image Bank/Getty Images Plus/Getty Images; TS Photography/Photographer's Choice/Getty Images Plus/Getty Images; Josie Iselin/Visuals Unlimited, Inc./Getty Images; Jane Burton/Dorling Kindersley/Getty Images Plus/Getty Images; James A. Guilliam/Photolibrary/Getty Images Plus/Getty Images; MediaProduction/E+/Getty Images; cynoclub/iStock/Getty Images Plus/Getty Images; Tetra Images/Getty Images; ViewStock/Getty Images; indigojt/iStock/Getty Images Plus/ Getty Images; Agency Animal Picture/Stockbyte/Getty Images; stilllifephotographer/Stone/Getty Images Plus/Getty Images; dvoriankin/iStock/Getty Images Plus/Getty Images.

Designer: Chefer

The authors and publishers would like to thank the following illustrators:

Sara Lynn Cramb (Astound US) p. 8; Ana Djordjevic (Astound US) pp. 10–13, 15, 33–37, 46–49, 70–72, 74, 77; Alejandro Mila (Sylvie Poggio Artists Agency) pp. 14, 22, 27, 29, 56–57, 61, 62, 64, 66, 76, 79, 81.